Ice Q and As

A Century of Hockey Intelligence

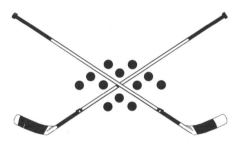

Other Books by Dan Diamond and Associates

NHL Official Guide & Record Book
Total Hockey: The Official Encyclopedia of the National Hockey League

Ice Q and As
A Century of Hockey Intelligence

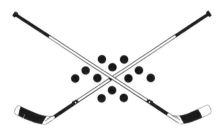

Eric Zweig and Dan Diamond

**Andrews McMeel
Publishing**

Kansas City

01 02 03 04 05 MVP 10 9 8 7 6 5 4 3 2 1

Library of Congress Cataloging-in-Publication Data

Diamond, Dan.
    Ice Q and As : a century of hockey intelligence / Dan Diamond and Eric Zweig.
        p. cm.
    ISBN 0-7407-1902-5 (pbk.)
    1. Hockey—Miscellanea. I. Zweig, Eric, 1963– II. Title.
    GV847 .D53 2001
    796.962—dc21

                                                2001022983

Book design and composition by Just Your Type

**For everyone
who cares for the game**

Contents

Ice Q and As

A Century of Hockey Intelligence

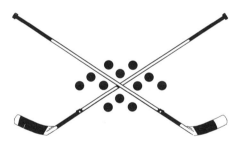

Chapter 1

Stanley Cup Now

The Stanley Cup was already entering its 25th season when the NHL was formed in 1917–18. It would take another 10 years before the trophy came under the league's exclusive control. But the exclusive control of the Stanley Cup by a single team was another matter altogether.

In the 15 years from 1927 to 1942, a total of eight different NHL teams won the Stanley Cup. However, the years that followed World War II would be characterized by a period of dynasties. Indeed, from 1945 to 1985 the total number of NHL teams that won the Stanley Cup was again eight. Of course, for much of that time the NHL had only six teams!

In recent years, NHL expansion has seen the league grow to 30 teams. Salaries have skyrocketed, and the modern economics of sports have made it almost impossible to keep a championship team together year after year. Care to take a guess at the total number of teams that won the Stanley Cup between 1990 and 2000?

You got it.

Eight.

So it would appear that the age of the hockey dynasty has come and gone. Yet the Stanley Cup's allure is more powerful than ever. For more than 100 years, the trophy has represented the highest level of accomplishment for a hockey player. It has been a talisman for the game, a focal point for players and fans alike. Yet where dreams of Stanley Cup glory were once reserved for Canadian kids on cold winter nights, today a boy—or a girl—wishing to become a hockey champion might be growing up anywhere from Anaheim to Asia, and all points in between.

For the first time since 1933 and 1934, back-to-back Stanley Cup titles were won in overtime in 1999 and 2000. Who scored the winning goals in these two series and who were the goalies they beat?

In addition to Brett Hull, only one other player scored the Stanley Cup–winning goal in overtime during the 1990s. Name the player, his team, and the goalie he scored against to win the Stanley Cup in 1996.

In 1997, the Detroit Red Wings won the Stanley Cup for the first time in 42 years. Goaltender Mike Vernon won the Conn Smythe Trophy that year, but was traded to the San Jose Sharks during the off-season. Twice before in Red Wings history the team had traded its number-one goaltender right after winning the Stanley Cup. Name these two future Hall of Fame netminders.

Brett Hull gave the Dallas Stars their first Stanley Cup victory in franchise history when he beat Dominik Hasek of the Buffalo Sabres at 14:51 of the third overtime period (54:51 of OT) on June 19, 1999. One year later, Jason Arnott of the New Jersey Devils beat the Stars' Ed Belfour at 8:20 of the second overtime period (28:20) on June 10, 2000. (By the way, Bill Cook scored against Toronto's Lorne Chabot to give the New York Rangers the Stanley Cup in 1933; Mush March beat Detroit's Wilf Cude to give Chicago the title in 1934.)

Uwe Krupp of the Colorado Avalanche scored against John Vanbiesbrouck of the Florida Panthers at 4:31 of triple overtime (44:31) on June 10, 1996.

After winning the Stanley Cup in 1950, the Red Wings traded Harry Lumley to Chicago to make room for Terry Sawchuk. Sawchuk helped Detroit win the Stanley Cup again in 1952, 1954, and 1955, but he was then sent to the Boston Bruins to open up a spot for Glenn Hall, another future Hall of Famer. Back in 1937, the Red Wings dealt away goaltender Earl Robertson after he helped them win the Stanley Cup, but Robertson had been a minor leaguer who was called up to replace injured starter Normie Smith.

Keith Primeau's goal at 12:01 of the fifth overtime period gave the Philadelphia Flyers a 2–1 victory over the Pittsburgh Penguins in an Eastern Conference Semifinal game on May 4, 2000. Primeau's goal ended the third-longest game in NHL history, and the longest game since the days of the Great Depression. Which players scored the goals that ended the two longest games in hockey history?

Only one game in the history of the Stanley Cup finals has lasted longer than the triple overtime victory of the Dallas Stars in 1999, albeit just 1:02 longer. This 1990 game between the Edmonton Oilers and Boston Bruins went until 15:43 of the third overtime period. Who scored the winning goal?

Who does not belong in this group of four players and why?

a) Wayne Gretzky   c) Kevin Lowe

b) Jari Kurri   d) Mark Messier

Ken Doraty of the Toronto Maple Leafs scored against Tiny Thompson of the Boston Bruins after 104:46 of overtime on April 3, 1933. The longest game in NHL history began on March 24, 1936, and ended on March 25 after a goal by Mud Bruneteau of the Detroit Red Wings when he beat Lorne Chabot of the Montreal Maroons after 116:30 of overtime. Both of these games, which required six overtime periods, were won by the score of 1–0!

Petr Klima's goal against former Oiler Andy Moog gave Edmonton a 3–2 victory. The Bruins outshot the Oilers 52–31 in this game.

a: Wayne Gretzky was traded before the Oilers won their fifth Stanley Cup title in 1990. The other three players all won five championships with the Oilers. Glenn Anderson, Grant Fuhr, Randy Gregg, and Charlie Huddy were also members of all five Oilers Cup–winning teams.

Who won the Conn Smythe Trophy as playoff MVP when the New York Rangers ended their 54-year Stanley Cup jinx in 1994?

Only six defensemen in NHL history have won the Conn Smythe Trophy as playoff MVP since it was first awarded in 1965. How many can you name?

What accomplishment is shared by each of these players?

a) Roger Crozier

b) Glenn Hall

c) Reggie Leach

d) Ron Hextall

Only three players in NHL history have scored at least 100 goals in the playoffs. Name them.

Though Mark Messier was the team's inspirational leader, defenseman Brian Leetch was awarded the Conn Smythe Trophy that year. Leetch led all playoff performers with 34 points (11 goals, 23 assists) that season, including 11 (five goals, six assists) in the seven-game final against Vancouver. Messier did win the Conn Smythe Trophy the first time the Oilers won the Stanley Cup, back in 1984.

Scott Stevens (2000), Brian Leetch (1994), Al MacInnis (1989), Larry Robinson (1978), Bobby Orr (1972 and 1970), and Serge Savard (1969).

Each of these four players won the Conn Smythe Trophy despite the fact that his team did not win the Stanley Cup. Crozier earned the honor with the Detroit Red Wings in 1966; Hall with the St. Louis Blues in 1968; Leach with the Philadelphia Flyers in 1976; and Hextall with the Flyers in 1987.

Wayne Gretzky (122 goals), Mark Messier (109 through the 2000-01 season), and Jari Kurri (106).

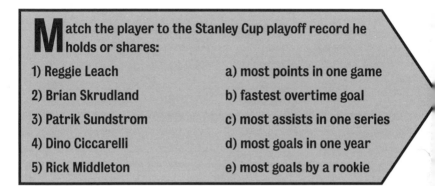

Match the player to the Stanley Cup playoff record he holds or shares:

1) Reggie Leach   a) most points in one game

2) Brian Skrudland   b) fastest overtime goal

3) Patrik Sundstrom   c) most assists in one series

4) Dino Ciccarelli   d) most goals in one year

5) Rick Middleton   e) most goals by a rookie

Match the coach with the team and year he won the Stanley Cup:

1) Jacques Lemaire   a) Pittsburgh   1995

2) Terry Crisp   b) Montreal   1991

3) Jean Perron   c) Calgary   1990

4) John Muckler   d) New Jersey   1989

5) Bob Johnson   e) Edmonton   1986

1-d: Leach shares the record of 19 goals in one playoff year with Jari Kurri. Leach did it for the Flyers in 1976; Kurri with the Oilers in 1985.

2-b: Skrudland scored for Montreal at nine seconds of overtime in game two of the 1986 Stanley Cup finals. The Canadiens beat Calgary 3–2.

3-a: Sundstrom shares the record of eight points in one game with Mario Lemieux. Sundstrom had three goals and five assists in a 10–4 New Jersey win over Washington in 1988. Lemieux had five goals and three assists in a 10–7 Penguins win over Philadelphia the following year.

4-e: Ciccarelli scored 14 goals in 19 games for Minnesota in 1981. His 21 points that year are also a rookie record.

5-c: Middleton and Wayne Gretzky share the record of 14 assists in one series. Middleton did it in a seven-game Bruins victory over Buffalo in 1983. Gretzky did it for Edmonton in six games against Chicago in 1985.

1-d, 1995: Lemaire's Devils surprised the Detroit Red Wings in four straight.

2-c, 1989: Crisp's Flames defeated the Montreal Canadiens in six games.

3-b, 1986: Perron guided the rookie-laden Canadiens to victory over Calgary.

4-e, 1990: Muckler helped the Oilers cap their dynasty with another win over Boston.

5-a, 1991: Johnson guided the Penguins to a six-game victory over Minnesota.

Since NHL expansion in 1967, only one team has reached the Stanley Cup Finals for three years in a row without winning at least one championship. Which team is it?

Three teams in NHL history have each won 11 consecutive playoff games in one season. Which of these teams is <u>not</u> one of them?

a) Edmonton, 1985   c) Pittsburgh, 1992

b) Chicago, 1992   d) Montreal, 1993

Only one player was a four-time Stanley Cup champion during the 1990s. Name him.

The St. Louis Blues reached the finals in 1967, 1968, and 1969 only to be swept in each series. In these years, the NHL's playoff format was devised to pit one of the new expansion teams against one of the "Original Six" clubs.

a: Though they once won 12 straight games over two seasons (1984 and 1985), the Oilers never won 11 consecutive playoff games in one year. Chicago won 11 straight to reach the Stanley Cup finals in 1992, only to be swept by Pittsburgh, whose four straight wins in that series gave them 11 wins in a row that year. Montreal won 11 straight in 1993 after losing their first two games in the playoffs.

Larry Murphy, who finished the 2000–01 season having played more games than any defenseman in NHL history, was a Stanley Cup champion with the Penguins in 1991 and 1992 and with the Detroit Red Wings in 1997 and 1998. Murphy is one of only six players to win multiple Stanley Cup championships with two teams. The others are Red Kelly (four with Detroit, four with Toronto), Dick Duff (two with Toronto, four with Montreal), Frank Mahovlich (four with Toronto, two with Montreal), Bob Goldham (two with Toronto, three with Detroit), and Bryan Trottier (four with the New York Islanders, two with Pittsburgh).

Stanley Cup Now

Since the NHL began competing for the Stanley Cup in 1918, only five players have ever scored four goals in one finals game. Which of these is not one of them?

a) Newsy Lalonde

d) Maurice Richard

b) Babe Dye

e) Mike Bossy

c) Ted Lindsay

Match the player to the Stanley Cup final series record he holds or shares:

1) Wayne Gretzky

a) most career points

2) Jean Beliveau

b) most career assists

3) Jari Kurri

c) most points in a seven-game series

4) Gordie Howe

d) most points, one game

5) Maurice Richard

e) most career goals

e: Mike Bossy never scored four goals in the Stanley Cup finals. Here's a look at when the others did it: Newsy Lalonde, March 22, 1919; Montreal 4 Seattle 2. Babe Dye, March 28, 1922; St. Pats 5 Vancouver 1. Ted Lindsay, April 5, 1955; Detroit 7 Montreal 1. Maurice Richard, April 6, 1957; Montreal 5 Boston 1.

1-b: Gretzky had 35 assists in 31 career games in the Stanley Cup finals. He had 16 goals and 30 assists in 26 games with the Oilers and two goals and five assists in five games with the Kings.

2-a: Beliveau had 30 goals and 32 assists for 62 points in 64 games in the finals. He is well ahead of Wayne Gretzky, who had 53 points in just 31 games and Gordie Howe, who had 50 points in 55 games.

3-d: Kurri is one of six players in NHL history to have collected five points in one game of the Stanley Cup finals. He had three goals and two assists in game two versus the Boston Bruins on May 17, 1990, a game the Oilers won 7–2. Eddie Bush (in 1942), Syl Apps (1942), Don Metz (1942), Sid Abel (1943), and Toe Blake (1944) also had five points in one finals game.

4-c: Howe had five goals and seven assists in Detroit's seven-game victory over the Montreal Canadiens in 1955. The record for most points in a final series of any length is 13, set by Wayne Gretzky in 1988 when the Oilers beat the Bruins in four games plus a suspended game.

5-e: Richard scored 34 goals in 59 career games in the Stanley Cup finals. Only two other players in NHL history came within 10 goals of the Rocket's record: Jean Beliveau, who scored 30 times, and Bernie Geoffrion, who had 24.

Put the following NHL players in order of Stanley Cup victories, starting with the most:

a) Bryan Trottier

b) Gordie Howe

c) Guy Lafleur

d) Bobby Orr

Put the following NHL coaches in order of Stanley Cup victories, starting with the most:

a) Hap Day

b) Glen Sather

c) Mike Keenan

d) Toe Blake

When Scotty Bowman won the Stanley Cup with the Detroit Red Wings for the second straight time in 1998, he tied Toe Blake for the most coaching victories with eight. Bowman's teams have reached the finals 12 times compared to nine for Blake, but one man in NHL history has guided his club to the finals a record 16 times. Who is he?

a) Bryan Trottier, six, New York Islanders (1980, 1981, 1982, 1983), Pittsburgh (1991, 1992)

c) Guy Lafleur, five, Montreal (1973, 1976, 1977, 1978, 1979)

b) Gordie Howe, four, Detroit (1950, 1952, 1954, 1955)

d) Bobby Orr, two, Boston (1970, 1972)

d) Toe Blake, eight, Montreal (1956, 1957, 1958, 1959, 1960, 1965, 1966, 1968)

a) Hap Day, five, Toronto (1942, 1945, 1947, 1948, 1949)

b) Glen Sather, four, Edmonton (1984, 1985, 1987, 1988)

c) Mike Keenan, one, New York Rangers (1994)

Dick Irvin coached in the NHL for 27 seasons between 1928 and 1957, and his teams made the playoffs 24 times. He first reached the finals as coach of the Chicago Blackhawks in 1931, then did it seven times with Toronto (1932, 1933, 1935, 1936, 1938, 1939, 1940) and eight times with Montreal (1944, 1946, 1947, 1951, 1952, 1953, 1954, 1955). He was a Stanley Cup champion in 1932, 1944, 1946, and 1953.

What feat was accomplished by Eric Desjardins, then of the Montreal Canadiens, in game two of the 1993 Stanley Cup finals?

Two players won the Stanley Cup with three different teams during the 1990s. Name them.

The Philadelphia Flyers became the first post-1967 expansion team to win the Stanley Cup when they defeated the Boston Bruins four games to two in 1974. The final game was a 1–0 victory for the Flyers. Bernie Parent earned the shutout. Who scored the goal?

a) Andre Dupont

b) Rick MacLeish

c) Bobby Clarke

d) Don Saleski

Eric Desjardins became the first defenseman in NHL history to record a hat trick in a Stanley Cup finals game. Desjardins scored two goals in regulation time, then netted the game winner 51 seconds into overtime as the Canadiens beat the Kings 4–3. Desjardins had tied the game with just 32 seconds left in regulation time after Marty McSorley was given a penalty for using a stick with an illegal curve.

Claude Lemieux and Mike Keane were teammates with both the 1993 Canadiens and the 1996 Colorado Avalanche. Keane was also a Stanley Cup champion with Dallas in 1999. The feisty Lemieux was a champion with the Devils in 1995. He was also a member of New Jersey's second Cup-winning club in 2000.

b: Rick MacLeish redirected an Andre Dupont shot past Bruins goalie Gilles Gilbert at 14:48 of the first period.

The New York Islanders beat four different teams when they won the Stanley Cup four years in a row. Who did they beat each year?

The Montreal Canadiens have won the Stanley Cup a record 24 times. Match the following Montreal players to their total number of Stanley Cup victories:

1) Maurice Richard   a) 11

2) Henri Richard   b) 8

3) Doug Harvey   c) 7

4) Serge Savard   d) 6

5) Bob Gainey   e) 5

The Islanders beat Philadelphia in six games in 1980. They beat Minnesota in five in 1981, then swept Vancouver in 1982 and Edmonton in 1983.

1-b: Maurice Richard won eight times (1944, 1946, 1953, 1956, 1957, 1958, 1959, 1960).

2-a: Henri Richard won 11 times (1956, 1957, 1958, 1959, 1960, 1965, 1966, 1968, 1969, 1971, 1973).

3-d: Harvey won six times (1953, 1956, 1957, 1958, 1959, 1960).

4-c: Savard won seven times (1968, 1969, 1973, 1976, 1977, 1978, 1979).

5-e: Gainey won five times (1976, 1977, 1978, 1979, 1986).
Two Montreal Canadiens players, Jean Beliveau and Yvan Cournoyer, were a part of 10 Stanley Cup winners, while Claude Provost was a nine-time champion. Jacques Lemaire joins Maurice Richard as an eight-time winner, while Jean-Guy Talbot matched Savard's total of seven victories.

(Note: Serge Savard was also a member of the Montreal Canadiens team that won the Stanley Cup in 1971, but he missed the majority of that season with a leg injury.)

Chapter 2

Stanley Cup Then

When the Stanley Cup was first presented to a team from the Montreal Amateur Athletic Association in 1893, the "modern" sport of hockey was less than 20 years old. The game was moved indoors off frozen lakes and rivers in the city of Montreal in 1875, and its popularity grew quickly. By the early 1890s, hockey was being played all across Canada and the Stanley Cup was donated to honor a national champion.

Due to the limits of 19th century technology, hockey was a game that could only be played in weather that was cold enough to sustain natural ice. In addition, train travel meant leagues had to be regional, not national. In order to make the Stanley Cup available to teams from all across the country during the winter months, the trophy could not belong to just one league. It had to be a challenge trophy. Winners of any league deemed worthy enough by a pair of trustees would be permitted to challenge the current Stanley Cup champion.

Hockey was strictly an amateur game through the turn of the 20th century, but as the prestige of winning the Stanley Cup increased, teams began paying for the best players they could find. By 1908, the game's top leagues were becoming professional, and so the top prize in the game became a professional trophy. By 1914 the pro game had provided two recognizable major leagues, so the challenge system was abandoned in favor of an annual World Series–like competition between the two league champions. When these leagues added American teams, the Stanley Cup trustees declared that the trophy would be symbolic of the world's professional hockey championship.

In 1926–27, the NHL emerged as the game's only major professional circuit. Since then, competition for the Stanley Cup has been held exclusively within the game's top league.

Who is the Stanley Cup named after?

The first all-American Stanley Cup final was played in 1929. Who were the teams involved?

For the first 10 years after the formation of the NHL in 1917–18, what two other professional leagues also competed for the Stanley Cup?

Frederick Arthur, Lord Stanley of Preston, was the son of a three-time Prime minister of England and himself a British member of Parliament. Stanley was appointed governor-general of Canada in 1888. Lord Kilcoursie, an aid of Stanley's, announced the governor-general's intention to donate a championship hockey trophy at a sports dinner in Ottawa on March 18, 1892. The trophy was first presented in 1893, though Lord Stanley had returned to England earlier that year.

The Boston Bruins beat the New York Rangers to win their first Stanley Cup title in 1929. The Bruins were led by coach and manager Art Ross and had a lineup that featured future Hall of Famers Dit Clapper, Cy Denneny, Mickey MacKay, Eddie Shore, Tiny Thompson, and Cooney Weiland. Frank Fredrickson, another future Hall of Famer, had also played with the Bruins that season.

The Pacific Coast Hockey Association and the Western Canada Hockey League (which was later known as the Western Hockey League) both battled the NHL for the Stanley Cup. The PCHA operated from 1911–12 through the 1923–24 season. Two of its teams then joined the WCHL, which had been in operation since 1921–22. In 1925–26, the WCHL dropped the "Canada" from its name when one of its teams (the Regina Capitals) moved to the United States (Portland, Oregon). Pro hockey in the west collapsed after that season, leaving the NHL as the only league in competition for the Stanley Cup.

What is the common bond shared by these four players?

a) Bob Turner

b) Don Marshall

c) Tom Johnson

d) Dickie Moore

Match the following names to the playoff feat they accomplished during the 1930s:

1) Bill Cook

2) Mel Hill

3) Tommy Gorman

4) Charlie Gardiner

5) Earl Robertson

a) two shutouts in the finals as a rookie

b) coached different teams to back-to-back Cups

c) recorded a shutout in his very last game

d) scored Cup-winning power-play goal in overtime

e) scored three overtime goals in one series

All four were members the Canadiens team that won five straight Stanley Cup titles from 1956 to 1960. Eight other players also suited up for all five teams. They are: Jean Beliveau, Bernie Geoffrion, Doug Harvey, Jacques Plante, Claude Provost, Henri Richard, Maurice Richard, and Jean-Guy Talbot.

1-d: Cook is the only player in history to score a Cup-winning power-play goal in overtime. He scored the OT winner in 1933 with two Leafs in the penalty box.

2-e: Hill earned the nickname "Sudden Death" when he scored three overtime goals for the Bruins during a 1939 semifinal series win over the Rangers. Hill remains the only player in history to score three OT goals in one series.

3-b: Gorman guided the Chicago Blackhawks to their first Stanley Cup title in 1934, only to be fired by temperamental team owner Frederic McLaughlin. Hired by the Montreal Maroons, he guided them to the 1935 Stanley Cup championship.

4-c: Gardiner was a star goaltender on a weak Chicago team for much of his brief career. Though plagued by severe headaches, he led the Blackhawks to the Stanley Cup in 1934, recording an overtime shutout in the clinching game. Sadly, he died of a brain hemorrhage two months later.

5-a: Robertson was a Red Wings farmhand when he was called up to Detroit during the 1937 playoffs. Playing in place of injured netminder Normie Smith, he posted shutouts in the last two games of the finals. Robertson would never play a regular-season game for Detroit, as he was traded to the New York Americans during the off-season.

The practice of engraving the team name of the Stanley Cup champion onto the trophy was one of the original terms laid down when Lord Stanley donated the trophy. When did teams first begin to formally include the names of all of their players?

a) 1893   c) 1915

b) 1907   d) 1924

By what name was the Stanley Cup originally known?

What is the common bond among the following:

a) John Sweetland   c) Cooper Smeaton

b) William Foran   d) Red Dutton

b: The first time that a team engraved the name of all of its players onto the Stanley Cup was 1907. The Montreal Wanderers had the names of all the players and the club executive carved into the Stanley Cup bowl after winning the trophy back from the Kenora Thistles. Among the 20 names listed is that of Lester Patrick. No other team engraved the name of its players on the trophy until 1915 when Lester's brother, Frank Patrick, had the names of the Vancouver Millionaires engraved inside the fluting of the bowl. However, not until the Montreal Canadiens won the Stanley Cup in 1924 did the practice of engraving player (and management) names on the trophy become an annual rite.

The Dominion Hockey Challenge Cup is the name that was formally engraved on the bowl of the trophy, though the Cup was almost instantly known by the name of its benefactor.

All four, along with Philip Dansken Ross, have served as Stanley Cup trustees. In the early days of the Stanley Cup, the trustees were responsible for overseeing the competition. After the NHL became the only league playing for the trophy in 1927, the position of trustee became largely symbolic—though the official terms of the deal that granted control of the Stanley Cup to the NHL on June 30, 1947, make it clear that the trophy does not belong to the league outright. The current trustees of the Stanley Cup are former NHL vice president Brian O'Neill and former Supreme Court of Canada Justice Willard Estey.

Which one of these Canadian cities never had a team that played a challenge series for the Stanley Cup?

a) Brandon, Manitoba   c) New Glasgow, Nova Scotia

b) Renfrew, Ontario   d) Moncton, New Brunswick

What was the first team from an American city to play for the Stanley Cup?

The only year in the history of Stanley Cup competition in which no champion was declared was 1919. Was there a connection between this event and the gambling scandal that plagued the 1919 World Series?

b: Though the Renfrew Creamery Kings (who would become known as the Millionaires) were instrumental in founding the National Hockey Association in 1909–10, no team from Renfrew ever played for the Stanley Cup. Brandon challenged the Ottawa Silver Seven in 1904, New Glasgow lost to the Montreal Wanderers in 1906, and Moncton was defeated by the Quebec Bulldogs in 1912.

The Pacific Coast Hockey Association moved a team to Portland, Oregon, for the 1914–15 season, and just one year later the Rosebuds (so named because Portland is "The Rose City") emerged as league champions. This gave them the right to play the champions of the eastern-based National Hockey Association for the Stanley Cup. However, the Portland team was defeated three games to two by the Montreal Canadiens in a best-of-five series. This was the first of the Canadiens' 24 Stanley Cup titles—one in the NHA and 23 in the NHL.

The 1919 Stanley Cup series between the Montreal Canadiens and Seattle Metropolitans was halted due to the epidemic of Spanish Influenza, which killed at least 25 million people worldwide between 1918 and 1920. With the series even at two wins and a tie apiece, so many Montreal players had become sick that the deciding game had to be canceled. On April 5, 1919, Canadiens star Joe Hall died in a Seattle hospital.

What was the first team from an American city to win the Stanley Cup?

The Ottawa Senators defeated the Boston Bruins in the first all-NHL Stanley Cup final in 1927. Put the following NHL teams in order of their first Stanley Cup victory, starting with the earliest:

a) Toronto Maple Leafs   c) Chicago Blackhawks

b) New York Rangers   d) Detroit Red Wings

What was the first NHL team to win the Stanley Cup?

The Seattle Metropolitans entered the PCHA for the 1915–16 season and, like the Rosebuds, became league champions in just their second year. Because of the distances involved during the era when the Stanley Cup was decided in a playoff between the champions of NHA and the PCHA, all of the games in a given year would be played in one location, the site alternating yearly between the champions of the east and the champions of the west. With the series scheduled for the west in 1917, Seattle became the first American city to play host to a Stanley Cup game. After dropping the series opener, the Mets rallied to defeat the Montreal Canadiens three games to one.

b) New York Rangers, 1928

a) Toronto Maple Leafs, 1932

c) Chicago Blackhawks, 1934

d) Detroit Red Wings, 1936

When the National Hockey Association was reorganized as the NHL in November 1917, the new league continued the NHA's Stanley Cup relationship with the PCHA. By capturing the first NHL title in 1917–18, the Toronto Arenas earned the right to host the Vancouver Millionaires for the Stanley Cup. Toronto took the best-of-five series with a 2–1 victory in game five.

Put these hockey teams in order of their first Stanley Cup victory, starting with the earliest:

a) Toronto Blueshirts

c) Montreal Victorias

b) Winnipeg Victorias

d) Quebec Bulldogs

For what on-ice feat is Ottawa Silver Seven star Frank McGee best remembered?

c) Montreal Victorias, 1895

b) Winnipeg Victorias, 1896

d) Quebec Bulldogs, 1912

a) Toronto Blueshirts, 1914

The Montreal Victorias unseated hockey's first Stanley Cup winners, the Montreal A.A.A., when they defeated them for the Amateur Hockey Association title in 1895. The Winnipeg Victorias became the first team to successfully challenge for the Cup when they defeated the Montreal Vics the following season. The Montreal team would win the Cup back with their own successful challenge later in the year. Quebec won the Stanley Cup as a member of the NHA in 1912. As league champions in 1914, the Toronto Blueshirts became the first NHA team to play a Stanley Cup series with the PCHA, sweeping the Victoria Aristocrats in a best-of-five series.

"One-Eyed" Frank McGee scored 14 goals in a single Stanley Cup game when the Silver Seven beat Dawson City 23–2 on January 16, 1905. One of early hockey's most prolific goal scorers, McGee lost the sight in his left eye when he was struck by the puck in a benefit game on March 21, 1900.

During the 1928 Stanley Cup final, the New York Rangers netminder was injured, forcing the 44-year-old coach and general manager to make an emergency appearance in goal. Who was the player that got hurt and who was the coach that filled in?

Put the following players in order of the number of times they played on a Stanley Cup championship team, starting with the fewest:

a) Howie Morenz

c) Bill Barilko

b) Eddie Shore

d) Doug Bentley

In the second period of game two between the Montreal Maroons and the New York Rangers, Rangers goalie Lorne Chabot was struck above the eye on a backhand shot from Nels Stewart and was rushed to the hospital. Though Ottawa Senators goalie Alex Connell was in the stands and agreed to fill in, the Maroons insisted that the Rangers had to use a player that was under contract to them, as the rules of the day stated. After considerable delay, coach Lester Patrick donned the pads and led the Rangers to a 2–1 victory in overtime. Prior to game three, an agreement was reached to allow the Rangers to use Joe Miller, a minor leaguer who had spent part of the season with the New York Americans. Miller led the Rangers to victory in five games. Though at the time, and for many years afterward, it was assumed that Lester Patrick had not been active for years and had never played goal, he had, in fact, spent a whole season on defense with the Victoria Cougars just two years before and had once played 10 minutes in goal for Victoria during the 1921–22 season.

d) Doug Bentley, none

b) Eddie Shore, two (1929, 1939)

a) Howie Morenz, three (1924, 1930, 1931)

c) Bill Barilko, four (1947, 1948, 1949, 1951)

What was the last non-NHL team to win the Stanley Cup?

Match the following team to its Stanley Cup accomplishment:

1) Detroit Red Wings

2) Toronto Maple Leafs

3) Chicago Blackhawks

4) Boston Bruins

5) Montreal Canadiens

a) rallied to win Cup from down three games to none

b) first sub-.500 team to win the Cup

c) first American team to win back-to-back titles

d) first to win back-to-back titles in the NHL era

e) first to sweep a best-of-seven series

The Victoria Cougars of the Western Canada Hockey League won the Stanley Cup in 1925. Originally members of the Pacific Coast Hockey Association, Victoria (formerly known as the Aristocrats) and the Vancouver Maroons (formerly the Millionaires) joined the WCHL for the 1924–25 season. With a lineup that included future Hockey Hall of Famers Frank Fredrickson, Jack Walker, Frank Foyston, and goalie Hap Holmes, the Cougars defeated a Montreal Canadiens team that boasted Howie Morenz, Aurel Joliat, Sprague Cleghorn, and Georges Vezina. The score in the best-of-five series was three games to one. Victoria returned to the Stanley Cup finals in 1926, but, in the last appearance by a non-NHL team, they were defeated by the Montreal Maroons.

1-c: Though they were the last of the NHL's so-called Original Six teams to win the Stanley Cup, Detroit became the first American team to win back-to-back titles in 1936 and 1937.

2-a: After dropping the first three games to Detroit in the 1942 Stanley Cup finals, the Leafs rallied to win four in a row. No other team in North American sports has ever rallied to win a championship after losing the first three games.

3-b: The Blackhawks snuck into the playoffs with a record of 14–25–9 in 1937–38, but they caught fire in the playoffs. Chicago's team featured eight American-born players, the most by a Stanley Cup champion until the 1995 New Jersey Devils.

4-e: The Stanley Cup finals were expanded from a best-of-five to a best-of-seven series in 1939. In 1941, the Bruins won four straight over the Red Wings.

5-d: The Canadiens defeated Chicago in 1930, then beat Boston in 1931. The Ottawa Senators had won back-to-back Stanley Cup titles in 1920 and 1921 when the NHL was still competing with the PCHA.

Match the following groups of Hall of Fame players with the early-era Stanley Cup team on which they starred:

1) Fred Scanlan, Art Farrell, Harry Trihey

a) Kenora Thistles

2) Harvey Pulford, Rat Westwick, Frank McGee

b) Montreal Wanderers

3) Moose Johnson, Hod Stuart, Lester Patrick

c) Vancouver Millionaires

4) Billy McGimsie, Si Griffis, Tommy Phillips

d) Montreal Shamrocks

5) Frank Patrick, Frank Nighbor, Cyclone Taylor

e) Ottawa Silver Seven

1-d: The Montreal Shamrocks won the Stanley Cup in 1899 and 1900. The trio of Scanlan, Farrell, and Trihey are credited with introducing teamwork and combination play to a sport that had previously stressed individual talent.

2-e: The Ottawa Silver Seven were Stanley Cup champions in 1903, 1904, and 1905. They won two more challenge series in January 1906 before finally surrendering their crown to the Montreal Wanderers.

3-b: After defeating the Ottawa Silver Seven in 1906, the Montreal Wanderers remained champions until 1908, though they lost the Cup briefly to the Kenora Thistles in a challenge in January 1907 before winning it back in March.

4-a: After challenging unsuccessfully in 1903 and 1905, the Kenora Thistles defeated the Montreal Wanderers, and Kenora became the smallest town ever to have a Stanley Cup–winning team. Formerly known as Rat Portage, the tiny town near the border of Ontario and Manitoba also had the shortest reign as Stanley Cup champions.

5-c: In 1915, the Vancouver Millionaires became the first PCHA team to win the Stanley Cup when they destroyed the Ottawa Senators by the scores of 6–2, 8–3, and 12–3.

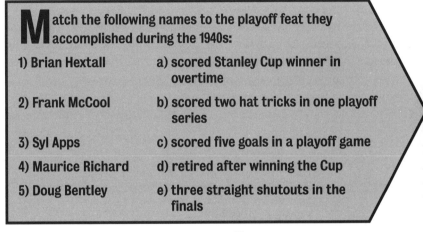

Match the following names to the playoff feat they accomplished during the 1940s:

1) Brian Hextall   a) scored Stanley Cup winner in overtime

2) Frank McCool   b) scored two hat tricks in one playoff series

3) Syl Apps   c) scored five goals in a playoff game

4) Maurice Richard   d) retired after winning the Cup

5) Doug Bentley   e) three straight shutouts in the finals

Who was the first woman to have her name engraved on the Stanley Cup?

1-a: Hextall scored the overtime winner for the Rangers over the Maple Leafs in 1940. It would be 54 years before another Ranger scored a Stanley Cup–winning goal!

2-e: McCool recorded three straight shutouts with the Maple Leafs to open the 1945 Stanley Cup final, though Toronto would lose the next three games before wrapping up the series in seven. A nervous goalie who was known as "Ulcers," McCool also won the Calder Memorial Trophy as rookie of the year in 1945, but played just one more season in the NHL.

3-d: Apps had announced prior to the 1947–48 season that the year would likely be his last. He topped 200 career goals (an impressive milestone at the time) during the last game of the regular season, and retired after the Leafs beat Detroit for the Stanley Cup.

4-c: Richard scored all five goals in a 5–1 win over Toronto in a semifinal game on March 23, 1944. He was the first to score five goals in an NHL playoff game since Newsy Lalonde in 1919. The only other players to score five goals in a playoff game are Darryl Sittler (1976), Reggie Leach (1976), and Mario Lemieux (1989).

5-b: Bentley recorded a pair of hat tricks for the Chicago Blackhawks during a semifinal series with Detroit in 1944. The feat was later matched by Norm Ullman (1964), Mark Messier (1983), and Mike Bossy (1983). In 1985, Jari Kurri had three hat tricks for the Oilers in a semifinal series with Chicago.

Marguerite Norris was the president of the Detroit Red Wings when they won the Cup in 1954. The Norris family owned the Red Wings from 1932 to 1982.

Match the following names to the playoff feat they accomplished during the 1950s:

1) Don Raleigh
2) Elmer Lach
3) Jacques Plante
4) Terry Sawchuk
5) Jean Beliveau

a) four shutouts in one playoff year
b) first of 14 career playoff shutouts
c) two overtime goals in one final series
d) scored the Stanley Cup winner in overtime
e) scored seven goals in one final series

Who does not belong in this group of four players and why?

a) Bill Barilko
b) Doug McKay
c) Tony Leswick
d) Pete Babando

1-c: Raleigh scored the overtime winners for the New York Rangers in games four and five of the 1950 Stanley Cup finals, but the Red Wings went on to win the series in seven. John LeClair (1993) is the only other player in NHL history to score two overtime goals in one Stanley Cup final.

2-d: Lach scored at 1:22 of overtime to give the Montreal Canadiens a 1–0 victory over Boston in the fifth and final game of the 1953 Stanley Cup final.

3-b: Plante blanked the Blackhawks 3–0 on April 4, 1953, for his first of 14 playoff shutouts. Plante broke Turk Broda's modern record of 13 with the St. Louis Blues on April 28, 1970. Clint Benedict's all-time record of 15 playoff shutouts was surpassed by Patrick Roy in 2000–01.

4-a: Sawchuk recorded four shutouts in just eight games during the 1952 playoffs as the Red Wings swept both the semifinals and finals to win the Stanley Cup.

5-e: Beliveau scored seven goals in just five games during the 1956 Stanley Cup finals, establishing a modern record for goals in a final series that was later equaled by Mike Bossy (1982) and Wayne Gretzky (1985).

b: Doug McKay's claim to fame is that he is the only player in history to play his only NHL game in the finals with a team that won the Stanley Cup. McKay played his one game with Detroit in 1950. The other three players all scored Stanley Cup–winning goals in overtime. Both Babando and Leswick scored their winning goals in game seven, making these two Red Wings the only players ever to accomplish that feat. Babando did it against the Rangers in a double-overtime thriller in 1950, while Leswick scored against the Canadiens in 1954. Barilko's overtime winner came for the Leafs in 1951. It would prove to be the last goal he ever scored because he was killed in a plane crash just a few months later.

Chapter 3

Hockey Hall of Fame

It is a place reserved for the greats of the game.

The highest honor an athlete can earn.

Induction into the Hall of Fame.

The Hockey Hall of Fame was established in 1943. Its mandate, then as now, was to preserve the history of the game of hockey and to honor those whose outstanding accomplishments have contributed to the development of the game. For a player to be eligible for the Hockey Hall of Fame, he must have been retired for at least three years—though there have been notable exceptions made to this rule in the past.

The first Hockey Hall of Fame inductions were made in 1945.

Twelve players were honored that year: Dan Bain, Hobey Baker, Russell Bowie, Charlie Gardiner, Eddie Gerard, Frank McGee, Howie Morenz, Tommy Phillips, Harvey Pulford, Art Ross, Hod Stuart, and Georges Vezina. In addition, Lord Stanley of Preston and Sir H. Montagu Allan were enshrined as builders. Today, more than 55 years later, and after more than a century of competitive play, just 319 men have become Honored Members of the Hockey Hall of Fame. The inductions of Denis Savard and Joe Mullen in the fall of 2000 brought the total number of players enshrined to 218. Another 87 men have been honored as "builders" (coaches, managers, executives, etc.), while 14 have been chosen for their contributions as referees and linesmen. All the great of the game are there: from Cyclone Taylor to Bobby Hull, from Eddie Shore to Bobby Orr, and from Gordie Howe to Wayne Gretzky.

Match the Hall of Famer to the team with which he
began his NHL career:

1) Phil Esposito   a) Boston Bruins

2) Tony Esposito   b) New York Rangers

3) Johnny Bower   c) Toronto Maple Leafs

4) Bernie Parent   d) Montreal Canadiens

5) Gerry Cheevers   e) Chicago Blackhawks

Put the following players in order of their induction
into the Hockey Hall of Fame, starting with the earliest:

a) Wayne Gretzky   c) Hap Day

b) Ken Dryden   d) Johnny Bower

1-e: Phil Esposito entered the NHL with Chicago in 1963–64. He was traded to the Bruins in a blockbuster deal after the 1966–67 season and later finished out his career with the New York Rangers.

2-d: Tony Esposito was signed by the Montreal Canadiens in 1967 and played 13 games with the club in 1968–69. After the season he was claimed by the Blackhawks in the Intra-League Draft.

3-b: Bower played a full season with the New York Rangers in 1953–54 and parts of two others before joining the Maple Leafs in 1958–59.

4-a: Parent played junior hockey in the Bruins system with the Niagara Falls Flyers and later spent parts of the 1965–66 and 1966–67 seasons in Boston. He was claimed by Philadelphia in the 1967 Expansion Draft.

5-c: Cheevers was Maple Leafs property when he was called up to Toronto to replace an injured Johnny Bower for games on December 2 and 3, 1961. He was later claimed by the Bruins in the 1965 Intra-League Draft.

c) Hap Day, 1961

d) Johnny Bower, 1976

b) Ken Dryden, 1983

a) Wayne Gretzky, 1999

Match the Hall of Famer to the team with which he finished his NHL career:

1) Bobby Orr
2) Bobby Hull
3) Doug Harvey
4) Serge Savard
5) Andy Bathgate

a) Winnipeg Jets
b) Chicago Blackhawks
c) St. Louis Blues
d) Pittsburgh Penguins
e) Hartford Whalers

Which of the following members of the Philadelphia teams that won back-to-back Stanley Cup titles in 1974 and 1975 is not an Honored Member of the Hockey Hall of Fame?

a) Fred Shero
b) Bernie Parent

c) Bobby Clarke
d) Bill Barber

1-b: After missing 70 games in 1975–76 while recovering from yet another knee operation, the Bruins allowed Orr to become a free agent. He signed with Chicago, but played only 26 games over the next three seasons.

2-e: Hull returned to the NHL with the Winnipeg Jets when four World Hockey Association teams were admitted to the NHL in 1979–80, but the Jets traded him to Hartford on February 27, 1980.

3-c: Harvey played 14 seasons with Montreal before later playing with the Rangers and Red Wings. He joined the St. Louis Blues for the playoffs in 1968 and played his final NHL season with the Blues the following year.

4-a: After 14-plus seasons with the Canadiens, Savard was going to retire after the 1980–81 campaign. The Jets talked him out of it and claimed him in the 1981 Waiver Draft. He played two seasons in Winnipeg.

5-d: Bathgate starred with the New York Rangers until he was traded to Toronto in 1964. He later played with Detroit, but his final NHL stop was Pittsburgh. He played with the Penguins in 1967–68 and again in 1970–71.

a: Coach Fred Shero is not a member of the Hall of Fame. Bernie Parent, who won the Conn Smythe Trophy as playoff MVP for both Flyers championships, was inducted in 1984. Bobby Clarke, the inspirational leader of the team, as well as the franchise's all-time leader in games (1,144), assists (852), and points (1,210), was inducted in 1987. Barber, who was a Stanley Cup champion during his first two full seasons in the NHL and went on to become the club s all-time leader with 420 goals, was inducted in 1990.

Ten players have had the three-year waiting period waived to allow for their immediate induction into the Hockey Hall of Fame. How many can you name?

When Gordie Howe ended his two-year retirement to play in the World Hockey Association (and later returned to the NHL for a final season in 1979–80), he became the first active Hall of Famer player in history. More recently, Hall of Famer Mario Lemieux returned to the game during the 2000–01 season. Only one other man has been active as a player after his induction. Who is he?

Which of the following coaches or executives is not an Honored Member of the Hockey Hall of Fame?

a) Bill Torrey

b) Glen Sather

c) Bill Wirtz

d) Lou Lamoriello

Wayne Gretzky (1999), Mario Lemieux (1997), Bobby Orr (1979), Gordie Howe (1972), Jean Beliveau (1972), Terry Sawchuk (1971), Red Kelly (1969), Ted Lindsay (1966), Maurice Richard (1961), and Dit Clapper (1947).

Many considered that Guy Lafleur had called it a career too soon when he retired from the Montreal Canadiens after playing 19 games in 1984–85. Shortly after his election to the Hockey Hall of Fame in 1988, Lafleur announced that he was going to make a comeback. He was signed by the New York Rangers for the 1988–89 season, then played two years with the Quebec Nordiques before calling it a career for keeps.

d: Though he has built the New Jersey Devils into a perennial powerhouse and won the Lester Patrick Trophy for his contributions to hockey in the United States, Lou Lamoriello is not a member of the Hockey Hall of Fame. As for the others, Bill Torrey was the architect of the New York Islanders dynasty and is currently the president of the Florida Panthers. Glen Sather was the longtime coach, G.M., and president of the Edmonton Oilers before joining the New York Rangers for the 2000–01 season. Bill Wirtz has been associated with the Blackhawks since his father, Arthur Wirtz, purchased the team with James D. Norris in 1952. He has been president of the club since 1966 and was the longtime chairman of the NHL Board of Governors.

Which of the following members of the Toronto teams that won three straight Stanley Cup titles from 1962 to 1964 is <u>not</u> an Honored Member of the Hockey Hall of Fame?

a) Tim Horton   c) Carl Brewer

b) Bob Pulford   d) Allan Stanley

Name the Honored Member of the Hall of Fame who is married to the daughter of another Hall of Famer.

Which three Honored Members of the Hockey Hall of Fame have played goal for the Toronto Maple Leafs and Detroit Red Wings?

c: Carl Brewer was an All-Star four times in his career, but he is not in the Hall of Fame. Horton, a six-time All-Star and four-time Stanley Cup champion, was inducted in 1977. Stanley, a three-time All-Star who, like Horton, also won the Stanley Cup in Toronto again in 1967, was inducted in 1981. Pulford, who was a great defensive forward for the Leafs' four Stanley Cup–winning teams of the 1960s, was inducted as a player in 1991.

Bernie Geoffrion married the daughter of Howie Morenz.

Harry Lumley was just 18 years old when he joined the Detroit Red Wings in 1943–44. He was traded to Chicago after the 1951–52 season and was dealt to Toronto two years later. Detroit had traded Lumley to make room for Terry Sawchuk, who, except for two seasons with the Bruins in 1956–57 and 1957–58, starred for the Red Wings through the 1963–64 season and was then acquired by the Maple Leafs. The other man who played goal for both teams was Charlie Conacher. Conacher was a top goal scorer during the 1930s, a time when teams only carried one goaltender. Goalies were required to serve their own penalties during this era, and twice during the 1933–34 season Conacher was called on to tend the Maple Leafs cage while Lorne Chabot served penalties. The following year, Conacher had another stint in the Toronto goal as an injury replacement for George Hainsworth. While with the Red Wings in 1938–39, Conacher filled in for Tiny Thompson when he was injured in a game.

Inducted in 1961, I am the only player in the Hockey Hall of Fame who was born in England (though I was raised in Winnipeg). I was on the move often during the pioneering days of the professional game until joining the Quebec Bulldogs in 1910–11. I helped them win the Stanley Cup in 1912 and 1913. When the Bulldogs chose not to operate a team during the NHL's first season of 1917–18, I was claimed by the Montreal Canadiens. Though best known as a tough guy, I was considered the top defenseman of my time. Who am I?

Match the Hall of Famer to his accomplishment:

1) Joe Mullen

2) Bobby Clarke

3) Stan Mikita

4) Bobby Orr

5) Bill Mosienko

a) first to win three major awards in one year

b) first expansion team player to top 100 points

c) scored a hat trick in 21 seconds

d) first American-born player to score 500 goals

e) won the Hart Trophy three years in a row

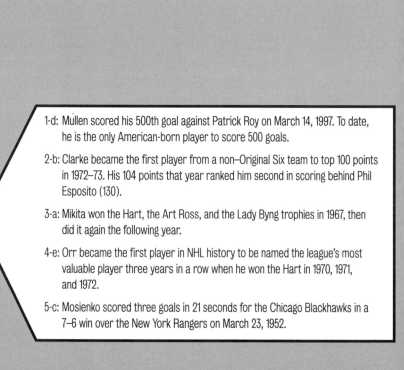

Joe Hall

1-d: Mullen scored his 500th goal against Patrick Roy on March 14, 1997. To date, he is the only American-born player to score 500 goals.

2-b: Clarke became the first player from a non–Original Six team to top 100 points in 1972–73. His 104 points that year ranked him second in scoring behind Phil Esposito (130).

3-a: Mikita won the Hart, the Art Ross, and the Lady Byng trophies in 1967, then did it again the following year.

4-e: Orr became the first player in NHL history to be named the league's most valuable player three years in a row when he won the Hart in 1970, 1971, and 1972.

5-c: Mosienko scored three goals in 21 seconds for the Chicago Blackhawks in a 7–6 win over the New York Rangers on March 23, 1952.

Wayne Gretzky has won the Hart Trophy as NHL MVP a record nine times, including eight in a row from 1980 to 1987. Put these other Hall of Famers in order of their Hart Trophy wins, starting with the most:

a) Maurice Richard

c) Eddie Shore

b) Gordie Howe

d) Howie Morenz

Two members of the Hockey Hall of Fame played with the WHA's Birmingham Bulls. One began his pro career with the club, the other ended it there. Both were high-scoring leftwingers. Name them.

Though I was an All-Star seven times in eight years between 1969–70 and 1977–78, I never won the Norris Trophy, overshadowed first by Bobby Orr and then by Denis Potvin. Like Orr, I would battle knee injuries throughout my career, though I was still able to play 17 seasons. I was inducted into the Hockey Hall of Fame in 1988. Who am I?

b) Gordie Howe, six (1952, 1953, 1957, 1958, 1960, 1963)

c) Eddie Shore, four (1933, 1935, 1936, 1938)

d) Howie Morenz, three (1928, 1931, 1932)

a) Maurice Richard, one (1947)

Frank Mahovlich joined the Toronto Toros of the WHA for the 1974–75 season after scoring 533 goals in an 18-year NHL career. Two years later, the Toros moved to Birmingham, where they became known as the Bulls. Mahovlich retired after the 1977–78 season, one year before Michel Goulet joined the team. An underage pro, Goulet and fellow rookies Gaston Gingras, Craig Hartsburg, Rob Ramage, Pat Riggin, and Rick Vaive were known as the "Baby Bulls." Goulet entered the NHL in 1979–80 and went on to score 548 goals in 15 NHL seasons with the Quebec Nordiques and the Chicago Blackhawks.

Brad Park

These two Hall of Famers are the only players in NHL history to be named all-stars as both forwards and defensemen.

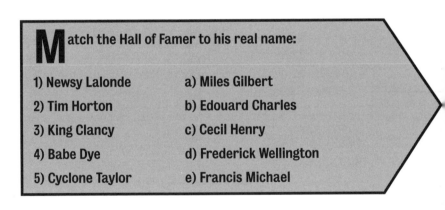

Match the Hall of Famer to his real name:

1) Newsy Lalonde   a) Miles Gilbert

2) Tim Horton   b) Edouard Charles

3) King Clancy   c) Cecil Henry

4) Babe Dye   d) Frederick Wellington

5) Cyclone Taylor   e) Francis Michael

Dit Clapper was the first man to play 20 years in the NHL, spending them all with the Boston Bruins. For 10 years, he was a top forward earning Second All-Star Team honors in 1931 and 1935. Converted to defense in 1937–38, he earned four selections to the First All-Star Team and one more to the Second. Rangers great Neil Colville was a member of the Second All-Star Team at center in 1939 and 1940 and on defense in 1948.

1-b: Newsy's nickname is said to have come from a childhood job in a newsprint factory.

2-a: According to stories, Horton's mother liked the names Miles and Gilbert. His father did not.

3-e: Clancy inherited his nickname from his father, a star rugby player in their hometown of Ottawa.

4-c: In addition to being a great goal scorer, Dye was also a baseball star (like Babe Ruth). He played minor league baseball throughout most of his NHL career.

5-d: According to legend, Taylor earned his nickname after a comment by Lord Grey (the governor-general of Canada who would soon donate a championship trophy to Canadian football) after his first game with the Ottawa Senators in 1907–08.

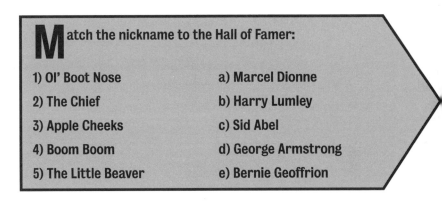

Match the nickname to the Hall of Famer:

1) Ol' Boot Nose
2) The Chief
3) Apple Cheeks
4) Boom Boom
5) The Little Beaver

a) Marcel Dionne
b) Harry Lumley
c) Sid Abel
d) George Armstrong
e) Bernie Geoffrion

Though only one spent the majority of his career with the team, eight Honored Members of the Hockey Hall of Fame have played with the Los Angeles Kings. How many can you name?

Wayne Gretzky broke Gordie Howe's career record for goals. Howe broke Maurice Richard's record. Who's record did Richard break?

1-c: Abel earned his nickname for obvious physical reasons.

2-d: Armstrong was known as "The Chief" as a tribute to his partial native heritage. Hall of Famer John Bucyk was called Chief for the same reason.

3-b: Lumley earned this nickname because of his ruddy complexion.

4-d: Geoffrion was called "Boom Boom" because of his slap shot.

5-a: Marcel Dionne's small size and large work ethic led to his nickname.

Marcel Dionne (1975–76 to 1986–87), Wayne Gretzky (1988–89 to 1995–96), Harry Howell (1970–71 to 1972–73), Bob Pulford (1970–71 to 1971–72), Larry Robinson (1989–90 to 1991–92), Terry Sawchuk (1967–68), Steve Shutt (1984–85), and Billy Smith (1971–72).

Richard scored his 325th career goal on November 8, 1952, breaking Nels Stewart's career record of 324, which had lasted since his retirement in 1940. Stewart had surpassed Howie Morenz when he scored his 271st career goal during the 1936–37 season. Stewart had entered the NHL with the Montreal Maroons in 1925–26. He promptly topped the league in scoring with 34 goals in 36 games, won the Hart Trophy as MVP, and led the second-year franchise to the Stanley Cup title. He scored a career-high 39 goals in 44 games during the 1929–30 season and won the Hart Trophy again. Stewart later played with the Boston Bruins and the New York Americans.

nducted into the Hall of Fame in 1982, I was called "the best center who ever played for me" by Punch Imlach. I led the NHL in goals scored with 42 in 1964–65, and when I jumped to the WHA in 1975–76, my 490 goals in 20 NHL seasons with Detroit and Toronto ranked eighth in history. Who am I?

he 1930s was a decade of great forward lines. Name the three sets of Hall of Fame players that made up Toronto's Kid Line, Boston's Kraut Line, and the Montreal Maroons' S-Line.

ine players who were members of all four Montreal Stanley Cup teams from 1976 to 1979 are also members of the Hall of Fame. How many can you name?

Norm Ullman

Leftwinger Busher Jackson, center Joe Primeau, and rightwinger Charlie Conacher were Toronto's Kid Line. Jackson and Conacher had won the Memorial Cup as junior teammates with the Toronto Marlboros in 1928–29 and went on to star together with the Maple Leafs on a line with Primeau beginning in 1929–30. Boston's Kraut Line of leftwinger Woody Dumart, center Milt Schmidt, and rightwinger Bobby Bauer had all grown up together around Kitchener, Ontario—an area known for its German heritage. They starred together with the Bruins in the late 1930s and '40s. Leftwinger Babe Siebert, center Nels Stewart, and rightwinger Hooley Smith were the top line for the Maroons from 1929–30 to 1931–32.

Yvan Cournoyer, Ken Dryden, Bob Gainey, Guy Lafleur, Guy Lapointe, Jacques Lemaire, Larry Robinson, Serge Savard, and Steve Shutt.

This Honored Member of the Hockey Hall of Fame was the first player to match Maurice Richard's feat of 50 goals in 50 games. Who is the player and who did he score the historic goal against?

Which one of these Hockey Hall of Famers was not a first-round draft choice?

a) Mike Bossy

c) Bryan Trottier

b) Lanny McDonald

d) Denis Potvin

Mike Bossy of the New York Islanders scored his 50th goal against Ron Grahame of the Quebec Nordiques with 1:29 remaining in the 50th game of the 1980–81 season. One of the most prolific scorers of all time, Bossy netted what was then a rookie record 53 goals in 1977–78 and went on to top 50 for nine straight seasons, a feat no one else has ever matched. Bossy fell short of 50 goals in only his final season of 1986–87 when injuries limited him to 38 goals in 63 games.

c: Bryan Trottier was selected by the Islanders in the second round (22nd overall) in 1974. The Islanders selected Clark Gillies with their first pick (fourth overall) that year. Potvin was picked first overall by the Islanders in 1973, the same year Toronto selected Lanny McDonald fourth overall. Mike Bossy was picked with the 15th selection in 1976. Potvin, Trottier, and Bossy all won the Calder Trophy for the Islanders in the 1970s and became the cornerstones of the club's four-year Stanley Cup dynasty in the early 1980s.

Chapter 4

All-Stars and Awards

The concept of honoring the game's top players is almost as old as hockey itself. In the 1890s and 1900s, sportswriters of the day would publish personal All-Star selections in their newspapers. The first known All-Star Game was played on January 2, 1908. The Hod Stuart Memorial Match raised funds for the family of the late Montreal Wanderers defenseman who had died in a diving accident on June 23, 1907.

Trophies to honor the NHL's top individual stars were first donated in the 1920s, beginning with the Hart Trophy for MVP in 1923–24, the Lady Byng Trophy for sportsmanlike play in 1924–25, and the Vezina Trophy for the top goaltender in 1926–27. The NHL began to name an All-Star Team after the 1930–31 season, but the league did not play its first All-Star Game until February 14, 1934. Like the 1908 Hod Stuart game, this was also a benefit match. It was played to cover the medical expenses and to provide additional funds for Toronto Maple Leafs forward Ace Bailey and his family. Bailey's career had ended when he suffered a fractured skull in a game at Boston on December 12, 1933. Similar benefits were later held after the death of Howie Morenz and Babe Siebert.

The concept of an annual NHL All-Star Game was born at the League's Board of Governors meeting in 1946. No game was played that year, but a year later the first official NHL All-Star Game (with proceeds going to the newly created Players' Pension Fund) was played at Maple Leaf Gardens on October 13, 1947. Throughout the history of the game, though, the honor of being selected to either the First or Second All-Star Team after the season has almost always been separate from playing in the All-Star Game.

First presented to the NHL's top goal scorer in 1998–99, the Maurice "Rocket" Richard Trophy is the most recent addition to the NHL's trophy case. List these other trophies in order of when they were first presented, starting with the most recent:

a) Jack Adams Award

c) Masterton Trophy

b) Jennings Trophy

d) Presidents' Trophy

Had there been a Rocket Richard Trophy in his day, Bobby Hull would have won it a record seven times. Put these other players in order of their goal-scoring titles, starting with the most:

a) Wayne Gretzky

c) Phil Esposito

b) Mike Bossy

d) Mario Lemieux

d) The Presidents' Trophy, given to the team that finishes first in the overall standings, was first presented in 1985–86.

b) The Jennings Trophy was first presented in 1981–82. Named in honor of long-time New York Rangers president William Jennings, the trophy is presented to the goalie or goalies on the team with the fewest goals scored against it. This used to be the criteria for the Vezina Trophy, which is now awarded to the goalie who is adjudged to be the best in a vote by NHL general managers.

a) The Jack Adams Award, named in honor of the longtime coach and general manager of the Detroit Red Wings, has been presented to the NHL's best coach since 1973–74. The winner is selected in a poll among members of the NHL Broadcasters' Association.

c) The Masterton Trophy has been presented to honor sportsmanship, perseverance, and dedication to hockey since 1967–68. It is named for Bill Masterton, a Minnesota North Stars player who died on January 15, 1968.

c) Esposito led the league in goals six times, doing it consecutively from 1969–70 to 1974–75. He set what was then an NHL record with 76 goals in 1970–71.

a) Gretzky led the league in goals five times. Beginning in 1981–82, when he shattered Espo's record with 92 goals, Gretzky led the league for four straight seasons, then did it again in 1986–87.

d) Lemieux led the league in back-to-back seasons in 1987–88 and 1988–89. He led the league a third time in 1995–96.

b) Bossy led the league in goals scored twice, netting 69 in 1978–79 and 68 in 1980–81.

Dominik Hasek is the only goaltender to win the Hart Trophy twice, doing it in back-to-back seasons in 1996–97 and 1997–98. Only four other goalies have ever been selected as the NHL's most valuable player. Name them.

The Vezina Trophy was presented to the NHL by the owners of the Montreal Canadiens in 1926–27 in memory of Georges Vezina, the Canadiens goaltender who collapsed during an NHL game on November 28, 1925, and died of tuberculosis a few months later. Montreal netminders have gone on to win the trophy more times than any other goalies. Name the Canadiens goaltenders who were the first to win the trophy three times in a row, four times in a row, and five times in a row.

This future Hockey Hall of Famer was the first player to win the Hart Trophy in 1923–24. He was also the first to win the Lady Byng Trophy when it was presented to the league in 1924–25, then won it again the following season. Who is this player?

Roy Worters, New York Americans, 1928–29

Chuck Rayner, New York Rangers, 1949–50

Al Rollins, Chicago Blackhawks, 1953–54

Jacques Plante, Montreal Canadiens, 1961–62

George Hainsworth won the Vezina Trophy the first three years it was presented. Bill Durnan won the award four times in a row from 1943–44 to 1946–47. After Turk Broda ended his streak, Durnan won the Vezina again in 1948–49 and 1949–50, giving him a record six victories in his seven-year NHL career. Jacques Plante won the Vezina Trophy five years in a row from 1955–56 to 1959–60. He equaled Durnan's record with his sixth win in 1961–62, then won it for a seventh time when he shared the honor with Glenn Hall as a member of the St. Louis Blues in 1968–69.

Frank Nighbor was a stylish center who was a great goal scorer and an excellent playmaker, as well as being one of early hockey's best defensive forwards. In addition to his individual honors, Nighbor was a five-time Stanley Cup champion, winning with the Vancouver Millionaires in 1915 and with the Ottawa Senators in 1920, 1921, 1923, and 1927.

Name the player who holds the record for the most points in one season by a player who was not named to the All-Star Team.

With 12 selections to the First Team and nine selections to the Second, Gordie Howe is the all-time leader with 21 selections to the NHL All-Star Team. Which of the following players is not the all-time leader at his position?

a) Ray Bourque

c) Wayne Gretzky

b) Bobby Hull

d) Terry Sawchuk

Which of these future NHL All-Stars was not a member of the NHL All-Rookie Team after his first full season?

a) Paul Kariya

c) Chris Pronger

b) Rob Blake

d) John LeClair

Steve Yzerman had 155 points in 1988–89 for the highest point total ever recorded by a player not named Gretzky or Lemieux. Unfortunately for Yzerman, Lemieux had a career-best 199 points that year (85 goals, 114 assists) and earned First All-Star Team honors at center. Gretzky had 168 points (54 goals, 114 assists) and was chosen to the Second Team. Yzerman finally earned All-Star honors for the first time when he was named to the First Team in 1999–2000.

d: Terry Sawchuk was a seven-time All-Star (three selections to the First Team), which ties him for third among goalies with Jacques Plante. Frank Brimsek was an eight-time All-Star (two First Teams, six Seconds), while Glenn Hall leads all goaltenders with 11 selections to the All-Star Team, including seven picks to the First Team. Ray Bourque leads all defensemen with 19 All-Star selections through the 2000–01 season, including 13 to the First Team. Wayne Gretzky was a 15-time All-Star at center (eight and seven), while Bobby Hull earned 12 berths (10 and two) at left wing.

d: John LeClair was not named to the All-Rookie Team when he was eligible in 1991–92. Kariya was named to the All-Rookie Team in 1994–95. Blake earned rookie honors in 1990–91. Pronger was a rookie star in 1993–94.

Match the player to the All-Star Game record he holds or shares:

1) Gordie Howe   a) most points in one game

2) Mario Lemieux   b) fastest two goals

3) Mats Naslund   c) most goals in one game

4) Wayne Gretzky   d) most games played

5) Owen Nolan   e) most assists in one game

Until the 1966–67 season, the NHL All-Star Game was played right before the beginning of the new season. In addition to the change in scheduling, the All-Star Game has undergone a number of format changes. How many different formats can you name?

1-d: Howe played in 22 All-Star Games in 25 seasons from 1947–48 through 1970–71, then played a 23rd time in the 1980 All-Star Game in Detroit.

2-a: Lemieux had six points (three goals, three assists) in the 1988 All-Star Game at St. Louis, leading the Wales Conference to a 6–5 overtime victory over the Campbell Conference.

3-e: Naslund had five assists for the Wales Conference in the same game that Lemieux had six points.

4-c: Gretzky had four goals in the 1983 All-Star Game, leading the Campbell Conference to a 9–3 win in Long Island. Three other players have since equaled the record, though Gretzky remains the only player to score all four of his goals in one period (the third).

5-b: Nolan scored two goals in eight seconds (18:54 and 19:02 of the second period) in the 1997 All-Star Game at San Jose. Still, his Western Conference team was defeated 11–7 by the Eastern Conference.

For the first four years (1947 to 1950), the defending Stanley Cup champions took on a team of NHL All-Stars. In 1951 and 1952, the All-Star Game featured the All-Star First Team (bolstered by players from the NHL's four American franchises) taking on the Second-Team All-Stars (bolstered by players from the two Canadian clubs). Again from 1953 to 1968, the Stanley Cup champions faced a team of All-Stars. From 1969 to 1973, the All-Star Game featured a team from the East Division against a team from the West. Further expansion by 1975 saw the game divided by conference, Wales versus Campbell. After division and conference names were changed to reflect geographic regions in 1993–94, the All-Star Game pitted the Eastern Conference against the Western Conference. In 1998, the format was changed to see NHL All-Stars from North America battle NHL All-Stars from the rest of the world.

Which of these future NHL All-Stars was <u>not</u> a member of the NHL All-Rookie Team after his first full season?

a) Dominik Hasek   c) Peter Forsberg

b) Pavel Bure   d) Nicklas Lidstrom

When Chris Pronger won the Hart Trophy in 1999–2000, he became the first defenseman to win the MVP award since Bobby Orr won it three times in a row from 1969–70 to 1971–72. Eddie Shore won the Hart Trophy four times in the 1930s, but only four other defensemen have ever been named most valuable player, and all of them did it before 1945. How many can you name?

Name the other three players who, in addition to Wayne Gretzky, have scored four goals in an All-Star Game.

b: Pavel Bure won the Calder Trophy as rookie of the year in 1991–92, but he was not voted to the All-Rookie Team. He had played all three forward positions that season, so voters weren't sure whether to list him at right wing, left wing, or center. Rules for the rookie team were later changed so that voters could select three forwards regardless of their positions. Hasek was named to the All-Rookie Team as a member of the Chicago Blackhawks in 1991-92. Detroit's Nicklas Lidstrom was also named to the team that year. Peter Forsberg earned rookie honors in 1994–95.

Babe Pratt, Toronto Maple Leafs, 1944

Tom Anderson, Brooklyn Americans, 1942

Ebbie Goodfellow, Detroit Red Wings, 1940

Babe Siebert, Montreal Canadiens, 1937

All but Anderson are Honored Members of the Hockey Hall of Fame.

Mario Lemieux scored four goals to lead the Wales Conference to a 12–7 victory over the Campbell Conference in front of his home crowd in Pittsburgh at the 1990 All-Star Game. Vincent Damphousse scored four to pace the Campbell Conference to an 11–5 victory at the 1991 All-Star Game in Chicago. Mike Gartner had four goals to help the Wales Conference score a 16–6 victory over the Campbell Conference in the highest-scoring All-Star Game in history at Montreal in 1993.

Ray Bourque's 19 selections to either the First or Second All-Star Team through the 2000–01 season trail only Gordie Howe's record of 21 All-Star selections. List the following Hall of Fame defensemen in order of the number of times they were selected to the NHL All-Star Team, staring with the most:

a) Doug Harvey

c) Eddie Shore

b) Bobby Orr

d) Earl Seibert

Three players won the Calder Trophy as rookie of the year after having already won the Stanley Cup the previous season. Can you name them?

a) Doug Harvey, 11 times (10 First Team, one Second)

d) Earl Seibert, 10 times (four First Team, six Second)

b) Bobby Orr, nine times (eight First Team, one Second)

c) Eddie Shore, eight times (seven First Team, one Second)

Eligibility rules for the Calder Trophy say that a player is to be considered a rookie if he has not yet played 25 games in any single preceding season nor six or more games in each of any two preceding seasons in a major professional league. Playoff games do not count. As such, Danny Grant, who had played 22 games for the championship Canadiens in 1967–68, plus 10 of 13 in the playoffs, was still considered a rookie when he was traded to the Minnesota North Stars for the 1968–69 season. Similarly, Tony Esposito played 13 games in goal for the Stanley Cup champion Canadiens in 1968–69 before being claimed by the Chicago Blackhawks in the Intra-League Draft after the season. He set a modern NHL record with 15 shutouts in his rookie season of 1969–70. Ken Dryden was called up to Montreal late in 1970–71. He played the final six games of the regular season, then all 20 games in the playoffs to not only lead the Canadiens to the Stanley Cup but also to win the Conn Smythe Trophy as playoff MVP. The following season he led the NHL with 39 wins and edged out Rick Martin, who had set a rookie record with 44 goals, for the Calder Trophy.

Which of these future Art Ross Trophy winners did not begin his NHL career by winning the Calder Trophy?

a) Bernie Geoffrion

c) Bobby Orr

b) Bobby Hull

d) Mario Lemieux

Which of these players was the first to win the Art Ross Trophy as the NHL's scoring champion?

a) Joe Malone

c) Elmer Lach

b) Howie Morenz

d) Gordie Howe

Wayne Gretzky won the Art Ross Trophy 10 times in his career, including seven seasons in a row from 1980–81 to 1986–87. Prior to Gretzky, Gordie Howe had established the NHL mark of winning six scoring titles. Put the following players in order of the number of times they won the Art Ross Trophy, starting with the fewest:

a) Mario Lemieux

c) Stan Mikita

b) Guy Lafleur

d) Phil Esposito

b: Bobby Hull was not the NHL's rookie of the year, finishing as runner-up to Frank Mahovlich in 1957–58. Geoffrion took rookie honors in 1951–52. Bobby Orr was rookie of the year in 1966–67, and Mario Lemieux earned the Calder Trophy in 1984–85.

c: Though Joe Malone won the first NHL scoring title in 1917–18, the Art Ross Trophy was not presented to the scoring champion until the 1947–48 season. Elmer Lach led the league that year with 61 points (30 goals, 31 assists) in 60 games. Lach, who centered the famed Punch Line with wingers Toe Blake and Maurice Richard, had previously led the league in scoring in 1944–45 with 80 points in 50 games. Lach set an NHL assists record with 54 that season as Richard became the first player in league history to score 50 goals.

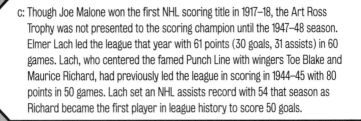

b) Guy Lafleur, three (1976, 1977, 1978)

c) Stan Mikita, four (1964, 1965, 1967, 1968)

d) Phil Esposito, five (1969, 1971, 1972, 1973, 1974)

a) Mario Lemieux, six (1988, 1989, 1992, 1993, 1996, 1997)

For the 30 NHL seasons prior to the first time the Art Ross Trophy was awarded, no player led the league in scoring more than twice. Eight players managed to accomplish the double feat, but only three of them did it in back-to-back seasons. Which one of these players is <u>not</u> one of them?

a) Howie Morenz

c) Sweeney Schriner

b) Charlie Conacher

d) Max Bentley

Two players in NHL history have dominated when it comes to consecutive trophy wins, winning the same awards for eight straight years. Who are the two players and what were the awards they won?

Which NHL player was given the original Lady Byng Trophy to keep after winning it seven times in eight seasons?

a: Howie Morenz led the NHL in scoring twice, but he did it in 1927–28 and 1930–31. Conacher was a back-to-back winner in 1933–34 and 1934–35, with Schriner then winning it consecutively in each of the next two seasons. Max Bentley won back-to-back scoring titles in 1945–46 and 1946–47. The other two-time scoring champions were Joe Malone (1917–18 and 1919–20), Newsy Lalonde (1918–19 and 1920–21), Babe Dye (1922–23 and 1924–25), and Bill Cook (1926–27 and 1923–33). Gordie Howe became the first player to win three scoring championships when he won three straight in the early 1950s. He made it four in a row in 1953–54.

Bobby Orr won the Norris Trophy as the NHL's best defenseman for eight straight seasons from 1967–68 to 1974–75. Denis Potvin ended his streak in 1975–76; injuries had limited Orr to just 10 games that season. Wayne Gretzky won the Hart Trophy eight years in a row from his rookie season of 1979–80 through 1986–87. Mario Lemieux ended his streak in 1987–88, though Gretzky was named MVP for the ninth time in 1988–89.

Frank Boucher of the New York Rangers was not only considered the game's most sportsmanlike player in a rough-and-tumble era, he was also the NHL's best playmaker. Centering a line with brothers Bill and Bun Cook, he led the league in assists three times and helped the Rangers win the Stanley Cup in 1928 and 1933. His stranglehold on the Lady Byng Trophy between 1927–28 and 1934–35 was broken only by Joe Primeau, who won the award in 1931–32. Boucher was runner-up in the voting that year.

The Norris Trophy for the NHL's best defenseman was presented to the league in 1953–54 in memory of the late James Norris, the former owner and president of the Detroit Red Wings. Who was the first player to win it?

Match the player to his accomplishment:

1) Bob Gainey   a) went nine seasons between trophy wins

2) Sergei Fedorov   b) first to win the Conn Smythe Trophy

3) Paul Coffey   c) first to win the Masterton Trophy

4) Jean Beliveau   d) named MVP and best defensive forward
                          in same season

5) Claude Provost   e) won Selke Trophy four years in a row

Red Wings great Red Kelly beat out Doug Harvey in voting for the Norris Trophy in 1954, though Harvey would win it for seven of the next eight years. Kelly also won the Lady Byng Trophy in 1954, the third of four times he would be named the league's most sportsmanlike player. Through the 2000–01 season, Kelly and Bill Quackenbush are the only defensemen in NHL history to win the Lady Byng Trophy.

1-e: Gainey won the Selke Trophy as the league's best defensive forward the first four years it was presented (1977–78 to 1980–81).

2-d: Fedorov is the only player to win the Hart Trophy and the Selke Trophy in the same season (1993–94). The only other man to win both trophies was Bobby Clarke, who won the Hart three times in the 1970s and the Selke in 1982–83.

3-a: Coffey won the Norris Trophy in 1984–85 and 1985–86, then went nine seasons before being named the best defenseman again in 1994–95. No one has ever had such a long gap in repeating a trophy win.

4-b: Beliveau won the Conn Smythe Trophy when it was first presented in 1965.

5-c: Provost won the Masterton Trophy when it was first presented in 1968.

Through the 2000–01 season, the only three-time winner of the Jack Adams Award as coach of the year earned the honor for leading three different teams. Name the man and the teams he coached.

Wayne Gretzky won the Hart Trophy and the Lady Byng Trophy after his first NHL season of 1979–80. Though he tied Marcel Dionne for the NHL scoring title, he did not win the Art Ross Trophy, nor did he win the Calder Trophy as rookie of the year. Why not?

Pat Burns first won the Jack Adams Award for guiding the Montreal Canadiens to 53 wins and 115 points in his first season as an NHL coach in 1988–89. Hired by Toronto in 1992–93, Burns led the Leafs to what were then club records with 44 wins and 99 points and won the Jack Adams Award for the second time. The Boston Bruins hired Burns in 1997–98 after the team recorded just 61 points and missed the playoffs for the first time in 29 years. He promptly led them to a 30-point improvement and won the Jack Adams Award for the record third time.

The rules regarding the Art Ross Trophy state that in the case of a tie, the trophy is awarded in the following manner: 1. Player with most goals. 2. Player with fewer games played. 3. Player scoring first goal of the season. Dionne and Gretzky both had 137 points, but Dionne had 53 goals to Gretzky's 51. Only once before in NHL history had the Art Ross Trophy been decided in this way: in 1961–62 when Andy Bathgate and Bobby Hull both had 84 points, but Hull had 50 goals to Bathgate's 28. As for the Calder Trophy, Gretzky was deemed ineligible because of the year he had played in the World Hockey Association.

Chapter 5

NHL Early Days

Professional hockey faced an uncertain future when the club owners of the National Hockey Association held a series of meetings in November 1917. The scarcity of players—and declining fan interest—caused by the First World War led to speculation that the NHA might suspend operations. The situation appeared to be coming to a head when the NHA owners met in Montreal on November 22. Four days later, on November 26, 1917, the NHA was no more. It had been replaced by the National Hockey League.

As it turned out, the reorganization of the NHA into the NHL had less to do with the effects of the war and more to do with getting rid of controversial Toronto owner Eddie Livingstone. In the

NHL, the Toronto franchise would be owned and operated by the Toronto Arena Gardens (aka the Mutual Street Arena). The Toronto Arenas, as the team became known, were charter members of the NHL along with the Ottawa Senators, the Montreal Canadiens, the Montreal Wanderers, and the Quebec Bulldogs.

But ridding themselves of Eddie Livingstone did not rid the NHL of the NHA's financial problems. Quebec elected not to operate a team for the inaugural season of 1917–18, and the Montreal Wanderers withdrew from the league after fire destroyed the Montreal Arena on January 2, 1918. The NHL was left with just three teams, but better times were ahead.

During the 1920s, the so-called Golden Age of Sports, the NHL expanded from a tiny regional league into a 10-team North American sports organization with a Canadian Division and an American Division. Though the NHL would later settle in as a six-team circuit, not only did the era of 1926–27 to 1941–42 see the game populated by some of its most colorful personalities, it also introduced new teams and new rules that would begin to define modern hockey.

Match the city to its NHL team nickname:

1) Hamilton   a) Quakers

2) Pittsburgh   b) Falcons

3) Philadelphia   c) Pirates

4) St. Louis   d) Tigers

5) Detroit   e) Eagles

What NHL scoring record that still stands did Joe Malone establish with the Quebec Bulldogs in 1919–20?

Early in the 2000–01 NHL season, New Jersey Devils teammates John Madden and Randy McKay each scored four goals in a 9–0 win over the Pittsburgh Penguins. No pair of teammates had accomplished this feat since the 1920s when two sets of Montreal Canadiens players did it. Can you name the four players involved?

1-d: Hamilton Tigers. They played in the NHL from 1920–21 to 1924–25.

2-c: Pittsburgh Pirates. They played in the NHL from 1925–26 to 1929–30.

3-a: Philadelphia Quakers. They played in the NHL in 1930–31.

4-e: St. Louis Eagles. They played in the NHL in 1934–35.

5-b: Detroit Falcons. When Detroit entered the NHL in 1926–27, they were known as the Cougars. They became the Falcons in 1930–31 and were renamed the Red Wings for the 1932–33 season.

Malone set an NHL record with seven goals in a 10–6 win over Toronto on January 31, 1920. Later in the year (March 10), he scored six goals in a 10–4 win over Ottawa. Malone led the league with 39 goals (and 49 points) in 1919–20, but the Bulldogs finished with just four wins and 20 losses during the 24-game season.

Newsy Lalonde and Harry Cameron each had four goals in a 16–3 win over the Quebec Bulldogs on March 3, 1920. The 16 goals scored by the Canadiens that night represent the highest single-game total in NHL history. On January 14, 1922, brothers Sprague and Odie Cleghorn both scored four goals in a 10–6 victory over the Hamilton Tigers.

Joe Malone of the Montreal Canadiens led the NHL in scoring during the first season of 1917–18. His goals scored that season stood as the NHL record until Maurice Richard scored 50 goals in 50 games in 1944–45. How many goals did Malone score?

I was the runner-up behind Joe Malone for the first NHL scoring title, and would finish second in scoring five times during the league's first nine years. I did manage to lead the league in scoring in 1923–24 and helped the Ottawa Senators win the Stanley Cup in 1920, 1921, 1923, and 1927. When I retired after the 1928–29 season, I was the NHL's career leader with 248 goals and 333 points. I was elected to the Hockey Hall of Fame in 1959. Who am I?

No Toronto Maple Leafs player has led the NHL in scoring since 1937–38, while no Rangers player has won the scoring title since 1941–42. Name the two Hall of Fame players who last accomplished these feats.

Malone scored 44 goals while playing just 20 games that season. A former NHA scoring champion when he starred with the Quebec Bulldogs, Malone was acquired by the Canadiens when Quebec chose not to operate a team. When the Bulldogs finally joined the NHL in 1919–20, Malone was returned to them.

Cy Denneny

Gordie Drillon of the Maple Leafs had a league-leading 52 points (26 goals, 26 assists) in 48 games in 1937–38. Bryan Hextall had 56 points (24, 32) in 48 games in 1941–42. Hextall's linemate Lynn Patrick led the league with 32 goals that season and is the last Rangers player to top the NHL in that category.

Which of the following American teams was the first to enter the NHL?

a) New York Rangers   c) Boston Bruins

b) Chicago Blackhawks   d) Detroit Red Wings

The first Olympic hockey tournament was held in conjunction with the 1920 Games in Antwerp, Belgium. Canada was represented by the Winnipeg Falcons, who won the gold medal. The Falcons' star player later turned pro with Victoria of the Pacific Coast Hockey Association and went on to play in the NHL with Detroit, Boston, and Pittsburgh. Name him.

This star of the 1924 Winter Olympics was considered to be the best amateur player in Canada. He was offered $30,000 to play with the Montreal Maroons, but decided not to turn pro and never played in the NHL. Who was he?

c: The Bruins entered the NHL, along with the Montreal Maroons, as part of the league's first expansion in 1924–25. The Rangers, Blackhawks, and Red Wings all entered the NHL in 1926–27 when the league grew to 10 teams following the collapse of the Western Hockey League. Two other American teams, the New York Americans and the Pittsburgh Pirates, had preceded those three teams into the NHL, entering the league in 1925–26.

Like almost every member of the Winnipeg Falcons, Frank Fredrickson was a first-generation Icelandic Canadian. He joined the Falcons in 1913–14 and, after military service as a pilot in the First World War, led the team to the Allan Cup and then Olympic gold in 1920. He went on to star for six seasons in Victoria, then played five seasons in the NHL. Fredrickson was elected to the Hockey Hall of Fame in 1958.

Harry "Moose" Watson was born in St. John's, Newfoundland, but raised in Winnipeg where he became a high school hockey star. Later moving to Toronto, he starred with the Granite Club team that won the Allan Cup in 1922 and 1923. As national senior amateur champions, the Toronto Granites represented Canada at the 1924 Winter Olympics in Chamonix, France. Watson scored 37 goals in five games as the Granites breezed to the gold medal. He rejected all offers to turn pro, choosing to continue playing (and coaching) in the amateur ranks. Watson died in 1957 and was elected to the Hockey Hall of Fame in 1962.

Match the player to his accomplishments in the NHL during the 1920s:

1) Corb Denneny

2) Punch Broadbent

3) Babe Dye

4) Alex Connell

5) Clint Benedict

a) scored nine goals in one Stanley Cup series

b) scored six goals in one game

c) recorded six consecutive shutouts

d) had league's best average for five straight years

e) scored in 16 consecutive games

Name the members of the Dynamite Line that helped the Boston Bruins rewrite the NHL record book after forward passing rules were introduced for the 1929–30 season.

1-b: Corb Denneny scored six goals for Toronto in a 10–3 win over Hamilton on January 26, 1921. Six weeks later, his brother Cy scored six goals against Hamilton in a 12–5 victory by the Senators.

2-e: Broadbent scored in 16 straight games for Ottawa during the 1921–22 season to establish a league record that still stands. He scored 27 goals during the streak and finished the year with a league-leading 32 goals and 46 points in 24 games.

3-a: Dye scored nine goals in five games to lead the Toronto St. Pats to a Stanley Cup victory over Vancouver of the Pacific Coast Hockey Association in 1921–22.

4-c: Connell recorded six straight shutouts for the Ottawa Senators during the 1927–28 season. At the time, however, forward passing was not allowed in the attacking zone.

5-d: Benedict led the NHL in goals-against average from 1918–19 to 1922–23. Although not as well remembered today as Georges Vezina, Benedict was arguably the better goaltender.

The Bruins combination of center Cooney Weiland and wingers Dit Clapper and Dutch Gainor helped the Bruins post a record of 38–5–1 in 1929–30 for an .875 winning percentage that is still the best in NHL history. Weiland led the league with 73 points (43 goals, 30 assists) in 44 games to set a scoring record that would stand for 12 years. Clapper had 41 goals and 20 assists to rank second in goals and third in points, while Gainor finished tenth in scoring with 18 goals and 31 assists.

Which of the following stars of the 1920s and '30s did <u>not</u> play professionally in the Western Canada Hockey League before entering the NHL?

a) Eddie Shore   c) Dick Irvin

b) King Clancy   d) Bill Cook

Match the following NHL team with the team it later became:

1) Quebec Bulldogs   a) New York Americans

2) Hamilton Tigers   b) Brooklyn Americans

3) New York Americans   c) Hamilton Tigers

4) Ottawa Senators   d) Philadelphia Quakers

5) Pittsburgh Pirates   e) St. Louis Eagles

b: King Clancy played his entire pro career in the NHL, beginning with the Ottawa Senators in 1921–22. Clancy's trade to the Toronto Maple Leafs for two players and $35,000 on October 11, 1930, was considered the biggest trade in hockey history. Eddie Shore began his career with the Regina Caps in 1924–25 and also played with the Edmonton Eskimos before joining the Bruins. Bill Cook starred in Saskatoon before entering the NHL with the Rangers. Dick Irvin played in both the PCHA and the WCHL with Portland and Regina before he began his NHL career in Chicago.

1-c: The Bulldogs were bought by Hamilton interests and became the Tigers in 1920–21.

2-a: After the 1924–25 season, the Tigers franchise was purchased by New York interests and became the Americans.

3-b: After playing second fiddle for years behind the Rangers, the New York Americans became the Brooklyn Americans in 1941–42. The franchise folded after that season.

4-e: Though Ottawa had won four Stanley Cup titles in the 1920s, U.S. expansion had left them as by far the NHL's smallest market in the 1930s. No longer able to make a go of it, the club transferred to St. Louis in 1934–35, but folded after the season.

5-d: The stock market crash of 1929 hit the steel industry of Pittsburgh hard, so the Pirates moved to Philadelphia after the 1929–30 season. The Quakers were a dismal 4–36–4 in 1930–31, and the franchise suspended operations.

What team was responsible for the NHL's first players' strike in 1924–25?

Name the goalie who established the NHL record of 22 shutouts in 1928–29.

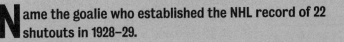

For the first 18 seasons of the NHL, every player who led the league in scoring had more goals than assists. Who was the first player to lead the league with more assists than goals?

The Hamilton Tigers refused to participate in the 1925 playoffs unless each member of the team received $200. The NHL had expanded from four to six teams in 1924–25 and the schedule had been increased from 24 to 30 games. While players on most other teams had received raises or bonuses, the Tigers did not. Hamilton had finished in first place during the regular season, but the entire team was suspended by NHL president Frank Calder when the players refused to back down from their demands. The Montreal Canadiens were declared NHL champions (they lost the Stanley Cup to the Victoria Cougars) and the Hamilton franchise was soon sold to New York.

George Hainsworth had 22 shutouts in just 44 games with the Montreal Canadiens in 1928–29. He allowed only 43 goals for a 0.92 goals-against average, also a single-season record. The 1928–29 campaign marked the lowest-scoring season in NHL history, with an average of just 2.8 goals per game by both teams! The following season, the NHL changed the rules to allow forward passing in the attacking zone.

Sweeney Schriner had 19 goals and 26 assists in 48 games to win the NHL scoring title in 1935–36. He had 21 goals and 25 assists when he led the league again the following season. Assists had become much easier to come by during the 1930s after forward passing was permitted in all three zones.

Put the following legendary hockey arenas in order of when they opened, starting with the first:

a) Chicago Stadium   c) Boston Garden

b) Maple Leaf Gardens   d) Montreal Forum

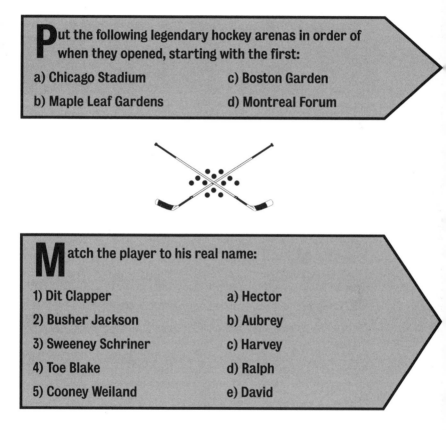

Match the player to his real name:

1) Dit Clapper   a) Hector

2) Busher Jackson   b) Aubrey

3) Sweeney Schriner   c) Harvey

4) Toe Blake   d) Ralph

5) Cooney Weiland   e) David

d) Montreal Forum; first game on November 29, 1924; Canadiens 7, Toronto 1*

c) Boston Garden; first game on November 20, 1928; Canadiens 1, Boston 0

a) Chicago Stadium; first game on December 16, 1929; Chicago 3, Pittsburgh 1

b) Maple Leaf Gardens; first game on November 12, 1931; Chicago 2, Toronto 1

As for the NHL's other legendary rinks, Madison Square Garden first installed ice for the New York Americans when they joined the NHL in 1925–26. The Detroit Olympia opened in 1927–28. The Detroit team had played across the border in Windsor, Ontario, when it entered the NHL in 1926–27.

*Though the Canadiens played the first game, the Forum was actually built for the Montreal Maroons. The Canadiens did not become full-time tenants until 1926–27.

1-b: Aubrey Victor "Dit" Clapper. He went by Victor as a boy, but his little brother pronounced it "Ditter."

2-c: Harvey Ralph "Busher" Jackson. Leafs trainer Tim Daly hung the tag on the cocky young Jackson, taking it from a character named Busher—a brash young baseball player—in a series of Ring Lardner stories.

3-e: David "Sweeney" Schriner. As a boy growing up in Calgary, Alberta, Schriner idolized a semipro baseball player named Bill Sweeney.

4-a: Hector "Toe" Blake. Similar to Dit Clapper, "Hec-toe" was easier to say than Hector.

5-d: Ralph "Cooney" Weiland.

Match the player to the feat he accomplished during the 1930s:

1) Rolly Huard   a) scored four goals in one period

2) Scotty Bowman   b) scored a hat trick in overtime

3) Ken Doraty   c) first to score on a penalty shot

4) Paul Thompson   d) first to score against his brother

5) Busher Jackson   e) scored in his only NHL game

Name the Toronto Maple Leafs defenseman who led the NHL in penalty minutes for eight straight seasons during the 1930s.

1-e: Huard was loaned to Toronto by the Buffalo Bisons as an injury replacement in December 1930. He played in just one game, but managed to score a goal. The only other player in NHL history to score a goal in his lone NHL appearance was Dean Morton, who did it with Detroit in 1989–90.

2-c: Bowman (not the NHL coach) of the St. Louis Eagles scored the NHL's first penalty shot goal against Alex Connell of the Montreal Maroons on November 13, 1934. Three days earlier, George Hainsworth of Toronto had stopped the Canadiens' Armand Mondou on the NHL's first penalty shot.

3-b: Doraty scored three overtime goals in a single game to give Toronto a 7–4 win over Ottawa on January 16, 1934. Since 1928–29, the NHL had been playing a full 10-minute overtime period when regular-season games ended in a tie.

4-d: Paul Thompson of Chicago scored against his future Hall of Fame brother Cecil "Tiny" Thompson of Boston on December 21, 1937.

5-a: Jackson set an NHL record that still stands when he scored four goals in the third period to lead Toronto past St. Louis 5–2 on November 20, 1934. The record has been equaled 10 times, most recently by Mario Lemieux on January 26, 1997.

Red Horner led the NHL in penalty minutes every season from 1932–33 to 1939–40, but he was no mere goon. Horner was one of the league's top blueliners and was Toronto's captain in 1938–39 and 1939–40.

Of the franchises that emerged from the era of 1926–27 to 1941–42 to become the NHL's "Original Six," only one had failed to finish first overall in the NHL standings at least once during this time period. Which team?

There have only been five times in NHL history when the scoring leader did not average at least one point per game played. Who was the last of these low-scoring scoring leaders?

What was the common link among these four goaltenders during the 1932–33 season?

a) George Hainsworth   c) Alex Connell

b) Charlie Gardiner   d) Roy Worters

The Chicago Blackhawks entered the NHL in 1926–27 but did not finish first overall until the 1966–67 season—the last season before expansion. According to legend, Pete Muldoon had vowed that the team would never finish in first place after he was fired as coach following the Blackhawks' inaugural season. In actual fact, "The Muldoon Curse" is thought to have been invented by sportswriters in 1941.

Toe Blake led the NHL with 47 points (24 goals, 23 assists) in 48 games in 1938–39. In addition to Blake and Sweeney Schriner, only Bill Cook and Ace Bailey have led the NHL with a scoring rate of less than a point per game. Both of them did it before passing rules were modernized. Cook had 33 goals and four assists in 44 games in 1926–27, and Bailey had 22 goals and 10 assists in 44 games in 1928–29.

Each of these goaltenders served as captain of his team, Hainsworth with the Canadiens, Gardiner with the Blackhawks, Connell with the Senators, and Worters with the Americans. Each of them was named captain in response to a new NHL rule that stated a captain must be on the ice at all times. Previously, goaltender John Ross Roach had served as captain of the Toronto St. Pats. The last goalie to serve as team captain was Bill Durnan, who shared the "C" with Elmer Lach during the 1947–48 season. Teams protested that when Durnan left his crease to protest calls it slowed down the pace of the game and gave the Canadiens unscheduled time-outs. Rules were changed prior to 1948–49 prohibiting goaltenders from being captains.

Match the star player of this era to the team with which he finished his career:

1) Hap Day   a) Toronto Maple Leafs

2) Busher Jackson   b) Montreal Canadiens

3) Howie Morenz   c) Montreal Maroons

4) Frank Nighbor   d) New York Americans

5) Lionel Conacher   e) Boston Bruins

Linemates finished one–two–three in the NHL scoring race in 1939–40. Name them.

1-d: After 13 years in Toronto, Day was sold to the New York Americans prior to the 1937–38 season. By the late 1930s, the Americans had become the dumping ground for a number of veterans who were past their prime.

2-e: The Leafs also dumped Jackson on the Americans in 1939–40, but they traded him to Boston two years later.

3-b: Morenz was swapped to Chicago in 1934–35, then to the Rangers in 1935–36, but returned to the Canadiens for what would prove to be his final season in 1936–37.

4-a: Like King Clancy a year later, Nighbor was a longtime Ottawa Senators star who was shipped to Toronto for financial reasons in 1929–30.

5-c: Though he also played with the Pirates, Americans, and Blackhawks, Conacher spent most of his NHL career with the Maroons. A star in many other sports as well, Conacher was named Canada's Athlete of the Half Century in 1950.

Milt Schmidt, the center of the Kraut Line, led the league with 22 goals and 30 assists for 52 points in 48 games. Woody Dumart was second with 43 points (22 goals, 21 assists). Bobby Bauer also had 43 points, but was ranked third because he only had 17 goals (and 26 assists). The only other linemates to finish one–two–three in scoring were Elmer Lach, Maurice Richard, and Toe Blake of the Punch Line in 1944–45 and Detroit's combination of Ted Lindsay, Sid Abel, and Gordie Howe in 1949–50.

Chapter 6

The Original Six

After the heady optimism of the Roaring Twenties had seen the NHL grow to 10 teams, the bleak years of the Great Depression saw franchises begin to fall by the wayside. Pittsburgh moved to Philadelphia after the 1929–30 season, but the team lasted just one more year. The Ottawa Senators became the St. Louis Eagles in 1934–35, then folded at season's end. The Maroons won the Stanley Cup in 1935, but the city of Montreal could no longer support two teams and the club disappeared after the 1937–38 season. The outbreak of World War II would eventually doom the New York Americans, and by 1942–43 the NHL was left with just six teams.

The NHL underwent more changes from 1926 to 1942 then it

would again until 1967 and the years beyond. But the "Original Six" teams that survived this era carried the NHL into a new period of unprecedented stability. Only about 100 players had steady jobs during this era, and to this day, the men who starred during the 25 years from 1942 to 1967 are remembered with particular awe and affection. Still, the game was changing. The introduction of the center ice red line in 1943–44 helped open up offensive play, as did the slap shot and curved sticks. In response, goaltenders began to wear masks.

If the 1920s were the "Golden Age of Sports," then for many, the Original Six era was the "Golden Age of Hockey." Seventy-game schedules meant that each of the teams faced the other five 14 times during the regular season, breeding a familiarity— and contempt—that is impossible to imagine today. The rivalries were fierce, the fan loyalties intense, and the game on the ice was unsurpassed in terms of skill and emotion.

Gordie Howe played 21 of his 26 NHL seasons during the Original Six era and leads all scorers with 649 goals. Maurice Richard is next with 544 in 18 years from 1942–43 to 1959–60. The following four players rank third to sixth. Put them in order of their goals scored in the era, starting with the most:

a) Bobby Hull   c) Jean Beliveau

b) Ted Lindsay   d) Bernie Geoffrion

Which two teams did not win the Stanley Cup during the entire Original Six era?

Who were the first pair of brothers to lead the NHL in scoring?

c) Jean Beliveau, 399 goals in 16 seasons

d) Bernie Geoffrion, 388 goals in 15 seasons

b) Ted Lindsay, 379 goals in 17 seasons

a) Bobby Hull, 370 goals in 10 seasons

The New York Rangers only made the playoffs seven times in 25 years and did not win the Cup during the Original Six era. Neither did the Bruins, who missed the playoffs for eight straight seasons from 1959–60 through 1966–67. The Montreal Canadiens won the Cup 10 times during the Original Six era, followed by Toronto who won it nine times. The Red Wings were five-time Stanley Cup champions during the era, while the Blackhawks managed to win it once, in 1960–61.

Max and Doug Bentley both won the scoring title as teammates with the Chicago Blackhawks. Doug tied Cooney Weiland's single-season record when he led the NHL in scoring with 73 points (33 goals, 40 assists) in 50 games in 1942–43. Max won back-to-back scoring titles in 1945–46 and 1946–47. A third Bentley named Reggie briefly joined his future Hall of Fame brothers for 11 games with the Blackhawks during the 1942–43 season.

Match the following groups of players to the famous line they were a part of:

1) Abel-Lindsay-Howe   a) Million-Dollar Line

2) Bentley-Bentley-Mosienko   b) Scooter Line

3) Mikita-Wharram-MacDonald   c) Uke Line

4) Bucyk-Horvath-Stasiuk   d) Pony Line

5) Hull-Hay-Balfour   e) Production Line

Wartime player shortages presented opportunities for many youngsters to crack NHL lineups in the early 1940s, including the youngest player in NHL history. Name him.

Who is the last player in NHL history to lead the league in scoring with more goals in a season than assists?

1-e: The Detroit trio of Sid Abel, Ted Lindsay, and Gordie Howe was first put together during the 1946–47 season. They were dubbed the Production Line in 1948–49.

2-d: The Bentley Brothers and Bill Mosienko were put together by Blackhawks coach Johnny Gottselig in 1945–46.

3-b: Stan Mikita, Kenny Wharram, and Ab McDonald played together with the Blackhawks between 1964 and 1969.

4-c: Bruins forwards John Bucyk, Bronco Horvath, and Vic Stasiuk were all of Ukrainian descent. They played together between 1957 and 1961.

5-a: Bobby Hull, Billy "Red" Hay, and Murray Balfour played together during the 1960s.

Aldo "Bep" Guidolin joined the Boston Bruins as a 16-year-old in 1942–43. Guidolin played on a line with 17-year-old Don Gallinger and 20-year-old Bill Shill. With the Kraut Line of Milt Schmidt, Woody Dumart, and Bobby Bauer all serving in the Royal Canadian Air Force, the Boston press dubbed this young threesome the Sprout Line.

Bobby Hull had a record total of 54 goals plus 43 assists when he led the NHL with a record 97 points in 1965–66. (The next year, Blackhawks teammate Stan Mikita equaled Hull's record of 97 points with 35 goals and a new single-season standard of 62 assists.)

Terry Sawchuk notched 100 of his record 103 career shutouts during the 18 years he played in the Original Six era. Which goalie ranks second to Sawchuk for this time period?

a) Glenn Hall

c) Johnny Bower

b) Harry Lumley

d) Bill Durnan

Put the following events in order of when they occurred, starting with the earliest:

a) Gordie Howe plays his rookie season

b) Maurice Richard scores 50 goals

c) Turk Broda wins his 300th game

d) season increases to 70 games

Which team invited Gordie Howe to his first NHL training camp in 1943?

b: Harry Lumley recorded 71 shutouts in 16 NHL seasons between 1943–44 and 1959–60. His 13 shutouts in 1953–54 were the highest single-season total of the era. Glenn Hall had 68 shutouts in 14 Original Six seasons. Durnan had 34 shutouts in just seven seasons, while Bower had 31 in 12 seasons. Jacques Plante had 63 shutouts during 13 seasons of the Original Six era.

b) Richard scored 50 goals in a 50-game season in 1944–45.

a) Howe entered the NHL in 1946–47.

d) The NHL season was increased from 50 to 60 games in 1946–47 and then to 70 games for the 1949–50 season.

c) Broda became the first NHL goalie to win 300 games on December 20, 1950.

Gordie Howe attended the New York Rangers training camp in Winnipeg as a 15-year-old in 1943, but the young boy was lonesome and homesick. The Rangers offered him a scholarship to Notre Dame College in his home province of Saskatchewan, but Howe only wanted to go home. A year later, traveling to Winnipeg with a trainload of his hockey-playing pals, Howe attended his first training camp with the Detroit Red Wings. The rest is hockey history.

Name the player who set an NHL record that still stands when he scored 15 seconds into his first NHL game on October 30, 1943. He later set an NHL record for the three fastest assists.

Four Montreal Canadiens players combined to win seven scoring titles during the Original Six era. Which one of these was <u>not</u> one of them?

a) Dickie Moore

b) Maurice Richard

c) Elmer Lach

d) Jean Beliveau

Of the seven players in NHL history to score six goals in a single game, only one managed to do it during the Original Six era. Which one of these four players was it?

a) Syd Howe

b) Gordie Howe

c) Vic Howe

d) Harry Howell

Gus Bodnar of the Toronto Maple Leafs scored against Ken McAuley of the New York Rangers just 15 seconds after the opening face-off of his first NHL game. He went on to score 22 goals and a rookie-record 40 assists and won the Calder Trophy. Later, as a member of the Chicago Blackhawks, Bodnar set up Bill Mosienko on all three goals when he scored a hat trick in 21 seconds on March 23, 1952.

Though he led the league in goals scored five times, Maurice Richard never won an NHL scoring title. Elmer Lach led the league in 1944–45 and 1947–48, Beliveau in 1955–56, and Moore in 1957–58 and 1958–59. The other Canadiens player to win a scoring title during this era was Bernie Geoffrion, who led the league in 1954–55 and 1960–61.

Syd Howe (no relation to Gordie) spent five-plus seasons with the Ottawa Senators, Philadelphia Quakers, Toronto Maple Leafs, and St. Louis Eagles before joining the Detroit Red Wings midway through the 1934–35 season. He would later score six goals in Detroit's 12–2 win over the Rangers on February 3, 1944. When he retired after the 1945–46 season, his 528 career points were the most in NHL history.

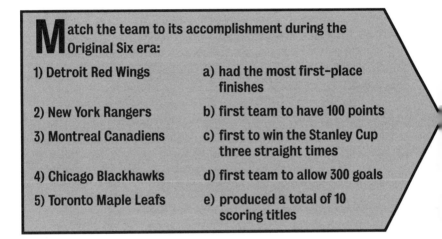

Match the team to its accomplishment during the Original Six era:

1) Detroit Red Wings   a) had the most first-place finishes

2) New York Rangers   b) first team to have 100 points

3) Montreal Canadiens   c) first to win the Stanley Cup three straight times

4) Chicago Blackhawks   d) first team to allow 300 goals

5) Toronto Maple Leafs   e) produced a total of 10 scoring titles

Ray Getliffe, Maurice Richard, Bernie Geoffrion, and Bobby Rousseau of the Montreal Canadiens all enjoyed five-goal games during the Original Six era. Name the era's only other five-goal scorer, a player who accomplished the feat as a rookie with the Toronto Maple Leafs in 1946–47.

1-b: One year after the schedule was expanded to 70 games, Detroit went 44–13–13 for 101 points in 1950–51. The Red Wings had 100 points (44–14–12) the following year. The Canadiens became the only other team to record 100 points during this era when they went 45–15–10 in 1955–56.

2-d: The Rangers allowed 310 goals during the 50-game season of 1943–44, setting a record for futility that would not be beaten until the California Golden Seals surrendered 320 goals in 78 games in 1970–71. Ken McAuley played all 50 games for the Rangers, posting a 6–39–5 record and a 6.24 goals-against average, the worst in history for anyone playing at least 30 games in one season.

3-a: The Canadiens finished atop the NHL standings in 12 of the 25 seasons during this era. Detroit finished first 10 times (including seven in a row from 1948–49 to 1954–55), Toronto twice (1947–48 and 1962–63), and Chicago once (1966–67).

4-e: Five Blackhawks players produced a total of 10 scoring titles during the era: Doug Bentley (one), Max Bentley (two), Roy Conacher (one), Bobby Hull (three), and Stan Mikita (three). Detroit and Montreal both produced seven scoring titles, while Boston had one.

5-c: The Leafs became the first NHL team to win the Stanley Cup three years in a row when they won in 1947, 1948, and 1949.

Future television analyst Howie Meeker scored five goals as a rookie in Toronto's 10–4 victory over Chicago on January 8, 1947. His five-goal performance still stands as a rookie record, equaled only by Don Murdoch of the New York Rangers in 1976–77.

Match the player to his accomplishment during the Original Six era:

1) Bobby Hull

2) Dickie Moore

3) Herb Cain

4) Bernie Geoffrion

5) Gordie Howe

a) set a new NHL scoring record with 82 points

b) set a new NHL scoring record with 95 points

c) set a new NHL scoring record with 96 points

d) second player to score 50 goals in a season

e) first player to score more than 50 goals

The Canadiens hold the NHL record for winning five consecutive Stanley Cup championships from 1956 to 1960, but what is the record for the most consecutive appearances in the Stanley Cup finals?

1-e: Hull, who had become the third player in history to score 50 goals in 1961–62, became the first to score 51 on March 12, 1966. He finished the 1965–66 season with 54 goals.

2-c: Moore had 41 goals and 55 assists for 96 points in 1958–59, breaking Gordie Howe's single-season record of 95.

3-a: With the introduction of the center ice red line in 1943–44 increasing the offense by allowing teams to pass the puck out of their own defensive end (i.e., across the blue line), Herb Cain of the Boston Bruins set a new scoring record with 82 points (36 goals, 46 assists) in just 50 games.

4-d: Bernie Geoffrion scored 50 goals during a 70-game season in 1960–61, matching the single-season record established by Maurice Richard in 50 games in 1944–45.

5-b: Howe broke Herb Cain's single-season scoring record when he totaled 86 points (43 goals, 43 assists) in 1950–51. Howe had 86 again (47 goals, 39 assists) the following year before setting a new record with 95 points (49 goals, 46 assists) in 1952–53.

The Canadiens had reached the finals for an amazing 10 straight seasons by the time they won their fifth consecutive championship. They made it every year from 1951 to 1960, though they lost to Toronto in 1951 and to Detroit in 1952, 1954, and 1955. They beat Boston in 1953, 1957, and 1958, Detroit in 1956, and Toronto in 1959 and 1960.

Put the following events in order, starting with the earliest:

a) Jacques Plante first wears a mask

b) Willie O'Ree breaks the color line

c) Gordie Howe scores his 545th

d) Glenn Hall's streak ends at 502

The decision by Clarence Campbell to suspend Maurice Richard for the remaining three games of the 1954–55 season and all of the playoffs sparked a riot on St. Catherine Street on the night of March 17, 1955. Richard was suspended for punching a linesman following a stick-swinging incident with a Bruins player four nights earlier. Name the player and the linesman involved.

b) Willie O'Ree became the first black player in the NHL on January 18, 1958. He played with the Boston Bruins briefly in 1957–58 and 1960–61 as part of a pro career that lasted until 1978–79.

a) Jacques Plante first wore a mask in a game on November 1, 1959, after being hit in the face by a shot from Rangers star Andy Bathgate. (Though Plante was the first to popularize the mask, Clint Benedict had actually worn one briefly during the 1929–30 season.)

d) Glenn Hall played in an astounding 502 consecutive regular-season games in goal from 1955 until a back injury sidelined him on November 7, 1962. Counting playoffs, the streak reached 552 games.

c) Gordie Howe surpassed Maurice Richard as the NHL's all-time goal-scoring leader on November 10, 1963. He had already surpassed Richard as the NHL points leader back in 1959–60.

Boston defenseman Hal Laycoe opened a five-stitch cut with a high stick to Richard's head. Angered by the sight of his own blood, Richard attacked Laycoe. Linesman Cliff Thompson tried to subdue Richard and wound up with a black eye.

Match the defenseman to his accomplishment during the Original Six era:

1) Flash Hollett

2) Pierre Pilote

3) Bill Quackenbush

4) Doug Harvey

5) Tim Horton

a) led his team in playoff scoring

b) won the Norris Trophy as a player/coach

c) first to score 20 goals in a season

d) most points in one playoff year

e) first to play full season with no penalties

In addition to winning the Stanley Cup for five years in a row, Montreal led the NHL with the most goals for and the fewest goals against in every season from 1955–56 to 1959–60. A total of six different Montreal players combined for 15 individual trophy wins during this unprecedented run of success. Who was the only member of the Canadiens to win the Calder Trophy during this time?

1-c: Hollett, who had twice scored 19 goals with the Boston Bruins, scored 20 for the Detroit Red Wings in a 50-game season 1944–45. This remained a record for defensemen until Bobby Orr scored 21 in a 76-game season in 1968–69.

2-a: Pilote became the only defenseman of the era to lead his team in playoff scoring (three goals, 12 assists) when Chicago won the Stanley Cup in 1961. His 15 points tied Gordie Howe for the most in the postseason that year.

3-e: Quackenbush became the first defenseman to win the Lady Byng Trophy after he played the entire 60-game season without recording a penalty in 1948–49.

4-b: Harvey won the Norris Trophy for the seventh (and final) time as a player/coach with the New York Rangers in 1961–62.

5-d: Horton's 16 points (three goals, 13 assists) in 12 games during the 1962 playoffs were the most by a defenseman during this era. Horton set up Dick Duff for the Stanley Cup–winning goal that year.

Ralph Backstrom had two brief trials with the Canadiens before being named rookie of the year in 1958–59. He had a career-high 27 goals in 1961–62 and led the club with 65 points that year. Though he helped the Canadiens win six Stanley Cup titles in 12 full seasons with the team, Backstrom was never more than the number-three center behind Jean Beliveau and Henri Richard. He was traded to the Los Angeles Kings in 1970–71 in a deal that helped the Canadiens land Guy Lafleur as 1971's number-one draft pick.

Gordie Howe was the Red Wings' top scorer 14 times in 16 years from 1950–51 to 1965–66. He led the club for nine years in a row from 1955–56 to 1963–64. What other player led his team in scoring for eight straight seasons during the Original Six era?

a) Frank Mahovlich   c) Bobby Hull

b) John Bucyk   d) Andy Bathgate

After being named the new general manager of the Toronto Maple Leafs in 1958–59, Punch Imlach soon hired himself as the club's head coach. Who was the man that Imlach replaced behind the bench?

a) Howie Meeker   c) King Clancy

b) Billy Reay   d) John McLellan

One of Punch Imlach's best moves as general manager in Toronto was to acquire Red Kelly from the Red Wings and convert him from defense to center. But before he was sent to Toronto, Detroit G.M. Jack Adams had tried to ship Kelly to what team?

d: Andy Bathgate was the Rangers' top scorer every season from 1955–56 to 1962–63. No other player during this era led his team in scoring for more than three consecutive years.

Punch Imlach replaced Billy Reay, who struggled for less than two seasons in Toronto but later went on to be one of the winningest coaches in NHL history (542 victories) with the Chicago Blackhawks. Reay had succeeded Howie Meeker behind the bench in 1957–58. Meeker had taken over from King Clancy in 1956–57. John McLellan would replace Imlach behind the Leafs bench in 1968–69.

Kelly and Billy McNeill were traded to the New York Rangers for Bill Gadsby and Eddie Shack on February 5, 1960, but the deal was voided when both Kelly and McNeill refused to report. Five days later, Kelly was sent to Toronto for Marc Reaume. He would go on to help Toronto win four Stanley Cup titles in the 1960s, adding them to the four he won with Detroit during the '50s. Kelly's eight Stanley Cup championships match the number of goals Reaume scored over parts of 10 seasons in the NHL.

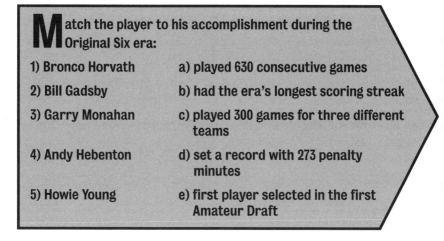

Match the player to his accomplishment during the Original Six era:

1) Bronco Horvath   a) played 630 consecutive games

2) Bill Gadsby   b) had the era's longest scoring streak

3) Garry Monahan   c) played 300 games for three different teams

4) Andy Hebenton   d) set a record with 273 penalty minutes

5) Howie Young   e) first player selected in the first Amateur Draft

Three players who began their careers during the Original Six era were still active in the NHL as late as the 1982–83 season. Which of these players was <u>not</u> one of them?

a) Serge Savard   c) Wayne Cashman

b) Carol Vadnais   d) Phil Esposito

1-b: Horvath had a point in 22 straight games during the 1959–60 season, the year he lost the scoring title to Bobby Hull by a single point (39–42–81 to 39–41–80).

2-c: Gadsby played his 300th game for Detroit on February 5, 1966. He had already played 300 with Chicago and the Rangers.

3-e: Monahan was selected first overall by Montreal in the 1963 Amateur Draft, though he didn't join the Canadiens until the 1967–68 season.

4-a: Hebenton was the Iron Man of the Original Six era, playing every single game throughout his nine-year career. When his minor league statistics are included, Hebenton's streak reaches 1,062 games. He had played 216 straight games in the minors before getting called up to the NHL, then 216 more after his NHL career ended in 1964. His streak finally ended during the 1967–68 season when he returned home to attend his father's funeral.

5-d: Young shattered Lou Fontinato's record of 202 penalty minutes in 1962–63.

d: Phil Esposito, whose NHL career began in 1963–64, called it a career after the 1980–81 season. Carol Vadnais broke in with the Montreal Canadiens in 1966–67 (11 games) and called it quits after the New Jersey Devils failed to make the playoffs in 1982–83. Serge Savard, who also broke in with the Canadiens in 1966–67 (two games) retired after a first-round playoff loss with the Winnipeg Jets in 1982–83. Wayne Cashman, who played one game for Boston in 1964–65 before becoming a regular after expansion, played with the Bruins until a second-round playoff defeat in 1982–83.

Chapter 7

Expansion

Though there had been a few rumblings in the 1940s and '50s—particularly from the city of Cleveland in 1952—the NHL gave very little thought to expansion until the 1960s. Major League Baseball was expanding. So was the National Football League. Finally, on February 8, 1966, NHL president Clarence Campbell announced that the league would double in size, from six to 12 teams, in 1967–68.

If any one person could be singled out as the driving force behind NHL expansion, it would be William Jennings of the New York Rangers. He submitted a memo to his fellow NHL governors in 1963 that called for two West Coast clubs to begin play in

1964–65. After the Jennings memo, the topic of expansion was on the agenda at every league meeting until the new franchises were finally announced.

The six clubs that were introduced by Campbell would be based in Los Angeles, San Francisco (Oakland), St. Louis, Pittsburgh, Philadelphia, and Minneapolis-St. Paul. They would all play together in the newly created West Division, while the Original Six clubs would form the East Division. The league's playoff format would ensure that one new team would play against one established club in the Stanley Cup final for the first three years.

Applications from Baltimore, Buffalo, and Vancouver were all rejected in 1966, though the latter two cities would join the NHL during the second round of expansion in 1970. New teams would be added again in 1972 and 1974, tripling the size of the NHL to 18 clubs (though it would later fall to 17). The admission of four teams from the World Hockey Association brought NHL membership to 21 clubs in 1979–80, and that number held fast until a new wave of expansion in the 1990s. By the start of the 2000–01 season, the NHL had grown to 30 clubs.

The NHL's first Expansion Draft was held on June 6, 1967. It consisted of 20 selections by each of the six new clubs. The first two rounds were limited to goaltenders. While most teams took at least one established veteran, the Philadelphia Flyers selected youngsters Bernie Parent and Doug Favell. Match the other sets of goaltenders to the team that selected them:

1) Oakland Seals

2) Los Angeles Kings

3) Minnesota North Stars

4) Pittsburgh Penguins

5) St. Louis Blues

a) Terry Sawchuk and Wayne Rutledge

b) Glenn Hall and Don Caley

c) Joe Daley and Roy Edwards

d) Charlie Hodge and Gary Smith

e) Cesare Maniago and Gary Bauman

Name the Tampa Bay player who set the record for goals (42) and points (86) on a first-year expansion team during the 1992–93 season.

1-d: Hodge was a veteran selected from Montreal. He spent three years with the Seals before being claimed by Vancouver in the 1970 Expansion Draft. Smith was a youngster from Toronto who lost a record 48 games with the Seals in 1970–71.

2-a: Sawchuk had just helped Toronto win the Stanley Cup. He only played one year for the Kings. Rutledge was a Rangers farmhand who spent three seasons with the Kings and later played six years in the WHA.

3-e: Maniago had played briefly with Toronto, Montreal, and the Rangers before going on to success with the North Stars. Bauman was claimed from Montreal, but played just 33 games in two seasons with Minnesota.

4-c: Daley was claimed from Detroit, but didn't play for the Penguins until the 1968–69 season. He later starred in the WHA with the Winnipeg Jets. Edwards was drafted from Chicago, but traded to Detroit before the season began.

5-b: Left unprotected by the Blackhawks, Hall proved to be the gem of the 1967 Expansion Draft, winning the Conn Smythe Trophy as playoff MVP in 1968 and sharing the Vezina Trophy with Jacques Plante in 1968–69. Caley, a former Red Wings prospect, played just one game for the Blues in 1967–68 and was traded to the Rangers. He never played in the NHL again.

Brian Bradley never had more than 19 goals and 48 points in any one season over seven years with Calgary, Vancouver, and Toronto until he was claimed from the Maple Leafs in the 1992 Expansion Draft. Though he would never match his 1992–93 numbers of 42 goals and 86 points, he would continue to perform effectively until an injury in 1997–98 ended his career.

In addition to Bernie Parent, three players selected by Philadelphia in the first Expansion Draft would go on to play for the Flyers teams that won back-to-back Stanley Cup championships. Which one of these players was <u>not</u> one of them?

a) Terry Crisp

c) Ed Van Impe

b) Gary Dornhoefer

d) Joe Watson

The Maple Leafs and Red Wings were involved in a blockbuster trade in 1967–68. Detroit picked up Frank Mahovlich, Pete Stemkowski, Garry Unger, and the rights to Carl Brewer. Who did Toronto get in return?

Which NHL expansion team had the roof blown off its arena late in the 1967–68 season?

a: Terry Crisp was claimed by St. Louis from Boston in the 1967 Expansion Draft and was later claimed by the New York Islanders in the 1972 Expansion Draft. The Islanders traded Crisp to Philadelphia during the 1972–73 season. As for the others, Dornhoefer and Watson were selected by the Flyers from Boston, while Van Impe was claimed from Chicago.

Norm Ullman, Paul Henderson, and Floyd Smith came to Toronto, but despite the big deal, both the Leafs and the Red Wings missed the playoffs in 1967–68 (though Toronto's 76 points were more than any of the expansion teams in the West Division). Ullman and Henderson were useful players in Toronto, but the Maple Leafs continued to struggle after expansion. They have not won the Stanley Cup since 1967. Detroit missed the playoffs 14 times in 16 years following expansion.

A late-winter storm damaged the roof of the Philadelphia Spectrum, forcing the Flyers to play home games on the road for the last 31 days of the schedule. Games were moved to Le Colisee in Quebec (where the Flyers had an American Hockey League farm club), as well as to Madison Square Garden and Maple Leaf Gardens. The Spectrum was repaired in time for the playoffs.

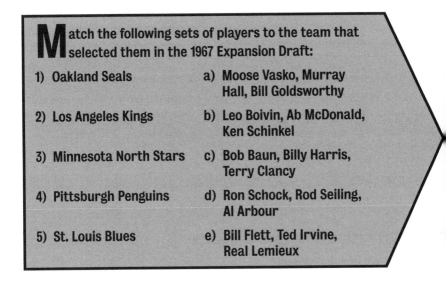

Match the following sets of players to the team that selected them in the 1967 Expansion Draft:

1) Oakland Seals

2) Los Angeles Kings

3) Minnesota North Stars

4) Pittsburgh Penguins

5) St. Louis Blues

a) Moose Vasko, Murray Hall, Bill Goldsworthy

b) Leo Boivin, Ab McDonald, Ken Schinkel

c) Bob Baun, Billy Harris, Terry Clancy

d) Ron Schock, Rod Seiling, Al Arbour

e) Bill Flett, Ted Irvine, Real Lemieux

One month before the first Expansion Draft, on May 15, 1967, the Chicago Blackhawks acquired Gilles Marotte, Pit Martin, and Jack Norris from the Bruins. What makes this deal so significant are the players Boston received in return. Can you name them?

1-c: Baun was a former Leaf who would later return to Toronto. Harris was a former Leaf who was drafted from Detroit. Clancy was a former Leafs prospect who would also return to Toronto. He is the son of King Clancy.

2-e: Flett played four-plus years with the Kings before being traded to Philadelphia. Irvine had played one game for Boston in 1963–64, but played 10 years after expansion. Lemieux had two stints with the Kings during an eight-year career.

3-a: Vasko and Hall were members of Chicago's 1961 Stanley Cup–winning team. Vasko came out of retirement to join the North Stars. Goldsworthy was a part-time Bruin who became Minnesota's biggest star.

4-b: Boivin was a future Hockey Hall of Famer who spent the last three years of a 19-year career with Pittsburgh and Minnesota. McDonald was a four-time Stanley Cup champion in Montreal and Chicago who played just one season with the Penguins. Schinkel was a spare part with the Rangers who became a consistent player over six seasons in Pittsburgh.

5-d: Schock was a former Bruin who would later go on to success with Pittsburgh. Seiling was traded back to the Rangers immediately after the draft and did not suit up for the Blues until 1976–77. Arbour was a journeyman defenseman who went on to coach the Blues and, later, the New York Islanders dynasty.

The Bruins acquired Phil Esposito, Ken Hodge, and Fred Stanfield. Boston had missed the playoffs for eight straight seasons entering the 1967–68 campaign, but these three players—along with Bobby Orr and longtime Bruin John Bucyk—would help lead Boston to two Stanley Cup titles in the next five years.

Though the Blues reached the Stanley Cup finals in 1968, they had only finished third in the West Division standings. Who finished first in the first year of expansion?

a) Los Angeles

b) Philadelphia

c) Minnesota

d) Pittsburgh

Name the two former Canadiens greats who led the Blues against Montreal in the 1968 Stanley Cup finals.

The NHL season stretched to 76 games in 1968–69 (it had been 74 games long the year before) and produced the league's first 100-point scorer. In fact, three players topped 100 points in 1968–69. Which one of these players was <u>not</u> one of them?

a) Phil Esposito

b) Gordie Howe

c) Bobby Hull

d) Stan Mikita

b: Only six points separated the top five teams in the West Division in 1967–68. Philadelphia finished first with 73, followed by Los Angeles (72), St. Louis (70), and Minnesota (69). The Penguins finished fifth with 67 points and missed the playoffs. Only Oakland wasn't in contention, landing in the basement with 47 points.

Dickie Moore had retired after the 1962–63 season, but made a comeback in Toronto in 1964–65. After two more years away from the game, he was lured to St. Louis by Scotty Bowman midway through the 1967–68 season. Doug Harvey had been bouncing around the minors for most of the last five seasons when he joined the Blues in time for the playoffs. Another former Canadiens legend, Jacques Plante, was talked out of retirement to join the Blues in 1968–69.

d: Mikita had led the league in scoring for the fourth time in five years with 87 points in 1967–68. He had 97 points in 1968–69, but finished in fourth place. Phil Esposito topped the league with 126 points (49 goals, 77 assists), becoming the first to reach the 100-point plateau on March 2, 1969. Bobby Hull reached 100 on March 20 and finished with 107 points. (His 58 goals that year set a new NHL record.) A 41-year-old Gordie Howe reached the 100-point plateau on March 30, 1969, and finished his 23rd NHL season with 103 points.

Hockey Hall of Famer Lynn Patrick (son of Lester Patrick and father of Craig Patrick) was the first coach and general manager of the St. Louis Blues, though he turned over bench duties to rookie Scotty Bowman early in the season. Match the rest of these men to the expansion team they coached in 1967–68:

1) Oakland Seals   a) Keith Allen

2) Los Angeles Kings   b) Wren Blair

3) Minnesota North Stars   c) Red Kelly

4) Pittsburgh Penguins   d) Bert Olmstead

5) Philadelphia Flyers   e) Red Sullivan

After losing the Stanley Cup to the Montreal Canadiens in 1968 and 1969, the Blues were beaten by the Bruins in 1970. The picture of Bobby Orr flying through the air after scoring the Cup winner that season is one of the most famous images in hockey history. Can you name the player that tripped Orr, the goalie he scored against, and the Boston teammate that set him up?

1-d: Olmstead was the first coach of the Seals, but he was fired with 10 games left in the season and was replaced by Gordie Fashoway.

2-c: Kelly was acquired by the Kings one day after the Expansion Draft. He then retired as a player in order to become the coach. He served two years with the Kings, followed by four with Pittsburgh and four in Toronto.

3-b: Blair coached the North Stars for their first season and parts of the next two. He was also the club's general manager from 1967–68 through 1973–74.

4-e: Sullivan coached the Penguins for their first two seasons. He and Lynn Patrick were the only two expansion coaches with previous experience behind the bench. Sullivan had coached the Rangers in the mid-1960s.

5-a: Allen was the Flyers coach for the first two seasons before becoming general manager in 1969–70. He held that job through the 1982–83 season and continues to serve in the Flyers front office.

Orr's goal 40 seconds into overtime gave Boston a 4–3 win over St. Louis for a sweep of the 1970 Stanley Cup final. He was set up by Derek Sanderson and put the puck past Glenn Hall. The Blues defenseman who tripped him was Noel Picard.

Which expansion team joined the NHL with the New York Islanders in 1972–73?

Can you name the three brothers who played together in St. Louis? Which one was not a member of the team during its inaugural season?

What team set new NHL records for wins and points in 1968–69, only to miss the playoffs in 1969–70?

Name the four World Hockey Association franchises that were absorbed by the NHL in 1979–80 and the two remaining WHA teams that were paid to go out of business?

The Atlanta Flames posted a respectable 25–38–15 record in their first season of 1972–73 and made the playoffs in year two. However, they moved to Calgary in 1980–81. The Islanders were a dismal 12–60–6 in 1972–73, but were among the league's best teams by 1975–76.

Bob Plager entered the NHL with the New York Rangers in 1963–64 and was traded to St. Louis immediately after the Expansion Draft. Barclay Plager was a well-traveled minor leaguer who was sent to the Blues by the Rangers early in the 1967–68 season. Bill Plager entered the NHL with Minnesota in 1967–68. He was claimed by the Rangers after the season, and then dealt to the Blues.

The Montreal Canadiens had 46 wins (46–19–11) and 103 points in 1968–69 and went on to win the Stanley Cup. They missed the playoffs in 1969–70, even though their total of 92 points was higher than any West Division team. The Canadiens actually finished tied with New York, but were relegated to fifth place in the East Division because they had scored two less goals (246–244) than the Rangers. Toronto finished last in the East that year. To date, the 1969–70 season marks the only time that no Canadian team qualified for the NHL playoffs.

The Edmonton Oilers, Winnipeg Jets, Hartford Whalers, and Quebec Nordiques all entered the NHL from the WHA. The Cincinnati Stingers and the Birmingham Bulls were bought out. The Indianapolis Racers—Wayne Gretzky's first professional team—had also been part of the WHA's final season of 1978–79, but they folded in December. Gretzky had been traded to the Oilers on November 2, 1978.

When the Buffalo Sabres and Vancouver Canucks entered the NHL for the 1970–71 season, they were given the first two picks in the 1970 Amateur Draft. A spin of the wheel determined that the Sabres would get the first pick, and they took Gilbert Perreault. Who did Vancouver select second overall?

Beginning with Denis Potvin in 1973–74, the Islanders and Flames alternated Calder Trophy winners for five years. Put these four rookie-of-the-year winners in order of their selection, starting with the earliest:

a) Mike Bossy   c) Eric Vail

b) Bryan Trottier   d) Willi Plett

What was significant about the 1969–70 scoring race?

Dale Tallon was a highly touted junior defenseman who set a rookie record with 42 assists in 1970–71, but never lived up to expectations. While Perreault set rookie scoring records with 38 goals and 72 points to launch a 17-year Hall of Fame career spent entirely with the Sabres, Tallon played just three years in Vancouver. He later played with Chicago and Pittsburgh during a 10-year career.

c) Eric Vail, 1974–75

b) Bryan Trottier, 1975–76

d) Willi Plett, 1976–77

a) Mike Bossy, 1977–78

Bobby Orr became the first defenseman to lead the NHL in scoring with 120 points in 1969–70. His 33 goals smashed his own record of 21 by a blueliner set the season before, while his 87 assists broke teammate Phil Esposito's one-year-old NHL mark. In addition to winning the Art Ross Trophy, Orr also won the Norris Trophy as best defenseman and the Hart as MVP. When he won the Conn Smythe Trophy as playoff MVP, he became the first player to win four major awards in one season.

Each of the top-10 scorers in 1967–68 had been a member of an Original Six team. Who became the first expansion team player to crack the top 10 in 1968–69?

When the Washington Capitals and Kansas City Scouts joined the NHL in 1974–75, the 18-team league split into two conferences (the Prince of Wales and the Clarence Campbell Conference) with two divisions in each. What were the names of the four new divisions and who were they named after?

Put the following players in order of where they were selected overall in the Entry Draft, starting with the highest choice. (Note: these players were not all selected in the same year.)

a) David Legwand

c) Rostislav Klesla

b) Patrik Stefan

d) Marian Gaborik

Red Berenson of the St. Louis Blues finished eighth in scoring with 82 points (35 goals, 47 assists) in 1968–69. On November 7, 1968, Berenson scored six goals in an 8–0 win at Philadelphia. He is the only player in NHL history to score six goals in a road game.

The Norris Division was named for longtime Red Wings owner James Norris. The Adams Division was named for original Boston Bruins owner Charles Adams. The Smythe Division was named after Conn Smythe, and the Patrick Division was named in honor of Lester Patrick.

b) Patrik Stefan was selected first overall by the Atlanta Thrashers in 1999.

a) David Legwand was selected second overall by the Nashville Predators in 1998.

d) Marian Gaborik was selected third overall by the Minnesota Wild in 2000.

c) Rostislav Klesla was selected fourth overall by the Columbus Blue Jackets in 2000.

Match the expansion team to its first-year record:

1) Washington Capitals   a) 8–67–5

2) San Jose Sharks   b) 10–70–4

3) Ottawa Senators   c) 17–58–5

4) Tampa Bay Lightning   d) 23–54–7

5) Florida Panthers   e) 33–34–17

Despite the geographic contradiction, both Buffalo and Vancouver were added to the East Division when they joined the NHL in 1970–71. Which Original Six squad was then moved into the West Division?

The price of an NHL expansion team in the 1990s was $50 million. What was the admission price when the first six expansion teams joined the league in 1967?

a) $1 million   c) $6 million

b) $2 million   d) $12 million

1-a: Eight wins are the fewest ever in a season of 70 games or more. Washington missed the playoffs in each of its first eight seasons.

2-c: San Jose won 17 games in its first year, but dipped to 11–71–2 in year two, setting a single-season record for the most losses in NHL history.

3-b: Ottawa recorded only one of its 10 wins on the road that year, going 1–41–0 and losing a record 38 straight on the opposition's home ice.

4-d: Tampa won 23 games and set an expansion team record with 245 goals.

5-e: Both Florida and Anaheim set expansion records with 33 wins in 1993–94. Florida's 83 points were also a record, while the Mighty Ducks' mark of 33–45–6 resulted in 71 points.

The Chicago Blackhawks had finished first in the East Division in 1969–70, but were moved into the West Division in 1970–71. They finished first in the West for three straight seasons.

The price of admission was $2 million per franchise in 1967. It was $6 million in 1970, 1972, and 1974.

Chapter 8

Hockey in the 1970s

At the start of the 1970s, the average salary in the NHL was $18,000. By the time the league entered the 1980s, it had risen to $108,000. Obviously, the game of hockey was in a time of transition. The NHL grew from 12 to 18 teams, then shrunk back to 17 after a number of franchises relocated. And for the first time since 1926, the NHL faced a challenge to its position as hockey's foremost professional league when the World Hockey Association opened for business in 1972–73.

With as many as 32 teams operating in the NHL and WHA by the mid-1970s, it became necessary to find new sources of hockey talent. As teams began recruiting around the globe, players from the United States and Western Europe—even the Iron Curtain countries—began to change the face of the game forever. The WHA introduced many of these new talents to professional hockey—including a skinny 17-year-old Canadian kid named Wayne Gretzky.

In the NHL, the 1970s were dominated by three teams: the Big Bad Bruins of Boston, the Broad Street Bullies of Philadelphia, and Les Glorieux —the Canadiens of Montreal. Boasting stars like Bobby Orr, Phil Esposito, Bobby Clarke, Ken Dryden, and Guy Lafleur, one of these three great teams would win the Stanley Cup every year during the decade. As often as not, it seemed that one of these teams was beating one of the other two to win the championship.

Like the late 1920s, the early 1970s was a time of great change in the NHL—only with longer hair and sideburns!

Borje Salming joined the Toronto Maple Leafs in 1973–74 and was the first European-trained player to become a star in the NHL. He was not, however, the first European-trained player in the league. Name the former Swedish star who played briefly with the New York Rangers in 1964–65.

Five different players led the NHL in goals scored during the 10 seasons from 1969–70 to 1978–79. How many can you name?

Only four different players led the NHL in scoring in the 10 seasons from 1969–70 to 1978–79. Phil Esposito did it four times, Guy Lafleur three, and Bobby Orr twice. Who won the decade's other scoring title?

A veteran of the Swedish national team who played at the Olympics in 1960 and 1964, Ulf Sterner was signed by the Rangers on October 1, 1964. He spent most of that season in the minors, but was called up to New York for four games. He returned to Sweden the following season. Swedish-born Juha Widing played junior hockey in Canada before joining the NHL with the Rangers in 1969–70. He went on to play eight years. The first European-trained player to play regularly in the NHL was Sweden's Thommie Bergman, who played with Detroit in 1972–73.

Phil Esposito led the league in goals for each of the first six years of the decade, scoring 43, 76, 66, 55, 68, and 61 goals over the course of those seasons. Reggie Leach led the league with 61 in 1975–76. Steve Shutt had 60 the following year, as did Guy Lafleur in 1977–78. Mike Bossy led the league with 69 goals in 1978–79.

Bryan Trottier of the New York Islanders led the NHL with 134 points (47 goals, 87 assists) in 1978–79. Trottier was the first player from a post-1967 expansion team to lead the NHL in scoring.

Four Boston Bruins topped 100 points in 1970–71 and finished 1–2–3–4 in NHL scoring. Name them.

Who were the members of the New York Rangers' GAG Line and what did the letters G-A-G stand for?

A total of 19 players combined for 31 50–goal seasons in the WHA, yet only one would go on to score 50 in the NHL in the 1980s, making him and Bobby Hull the only players to reach the milestone in both leagues. Name this talented 50–50 man.

Phil Esposito set new scoring records with 76 goals and 152 points in 78 games to finish first in scoring in 1970–71. Bobby Orr had a record 102 assists and finished second in scoring with 139 points. John Bucyk had 51 goals and 65 assists to finish third with 116 points. Ken Hodge, was fourth with 105 points (43 goals, 62 assists). In 1973–74, Esposito, Orr, Hodge and Wayne Cashman would finish 1–2–3–4 in scoring, but Cashman had only 89 points.

Center Jean Ratelle, leftwinger Vic Hadfield, and rightwinger Rod Gilbert made up New York's GAG Line, which stood for Goal-A-Game. The trio was at its best in 1971–72 when they finished 3–4–5 in scoring behind Phil Esposito and Bobby Orr. Hadfield was the first Ranger to score 50 goals that season. Ratelle had 46 in just 63 games, and Gilbert scored 43. Both Ratelle and Hadfield topped 100 points.

Blaine Stoughton had only scored 34 goals in parts of three NHL seasons when he jumped to the WHA in 1976–77 and scored 52 goals for the Cincinnati Stingers. Though he didn't even score 20 goals for the next two seasons, he scored 56 for the Hartford Whalers when they entered the NHL in 1979–80. Two years later, he had 52.

Match the player to his accomplishment during the 1970s:

1) Connie Madigan   a) only top-10 scorer to be traded in midseason

2) Michel Belhumeur   b) most appearances among the top-10 scorers

3) Jean Ratelle   c) stopped two penalty shots in one game

4) Bobby Clarke   d) scored 10 shorthand goals in one season

5) Marcel Dionne   e) made his NHL debut at age 38

How many goals and assists did Toronto's Darryl Sittler have when he set the NHL record of 10 points in a game on February 7, 1976? Who was the goalie that faced the onslaught?

1-e: Madigan was a longtime minor-leaguer who became the oldest rookie in NHL history when he joined the St. Louis Blues in 1972–73. He played only 20 games, then spent two more seasons in the minors before retiring.

2-c: Belhumeur stopped Jim Pappin and Stan Mikita on October 23, 1974, but Chicago still beat Washington 3–2. Belhumeur had been 9–7–3 with Philadelphia in 1972–73, but went 0–24–3 in Washington in 1974–75 and 0–5–1 in 1975–76.

3-a: Ratelle was traded from New York to Boston early in the 1975–76 season. He went on to finish the year with 105 points, sixth in the NHL.

4-b: Clarke finished among the top-10 scorers seven times in the 1970s. He was as high as second in 1972–73 and in 1975–76, when he had a career-high 119 points.

5-d: Dionne scored 10 shorthand goals for Detroit in 1974–75, a record at the time.

Darryl Sittler had six goals and four assists to lead Toronto to an 11–4 win over Boston. Bruins rookie Dave Reece was in net that night. It was the 14th and final appearance of his NHL career. Sittler would go one to become the first Leafs player with 100 points that season.

Match the player to the record he set during the 1970s:

1) Barry Beck   a) fastest to score 100 goals

2) Tom Bladon   b) most goals by a defenseman in one game

3) Rick Martin   c) most points by a defenseman in one game

4) Bryan Trottier   d) most goals by a rookie defenseman

5) Ian Turnbull   e) most points in a single period

Philadelphia's Rick MacLeish became the first player from a 1967 expansion team to score 50 goals when he reached the plateau in 1972–73. A total of 18 players recorded 31 50-goal seasons during the 1970s, yet only four of those players managed the feat with a 1970s expansion team. Which one of these four was <u>not</u> one of them?

a) Dennis Maruk   c) Danny Gare

b) Rick Martin   d) Guy Chouinard

1-d: Beck's record of 22 goals, set with the Colorado Rockies in 1977–78, was broken by Brian Leetch when he scored 23 in 1988–89.

2-c: Bladon broke Bobby Orr's record of seven points when he had four goals and four assists for Philadelphia on December 11, 1977. The record was later tied by Paul Coffey.

3-a: Martin set what was then a rookie record with 44 goals in 1971–72 and scored his 100th goal on December 9, 1973, after just 147 games. Mike Bossy would break both records, scoring 53 as a rookie (since broken) and netting 100 in 129 games.

4-e: Bryan Trottier had six points (three goals, three assists) in the second period as the Islanders beat the Rangers 9–4 on December 23, 1978.

5-b: Turnbull scored five goals (on five shots!) to lead the Leafs to a 9–1 rout of Detroit on February 2, 1977.

a: Although Dennis Maruk reached 50 goals twice with the Washington Capitals, he didn't do it until the 1980s. Rick Martin had 52 goals for Buffalo in 1973–74. He had 52 again in 1974–75. Danny Gare scored 50 for the Sabres the following year. Guy Chouinard had 50 for the Atlanta Flames in 1978–79. The fourth 50-goal scorer for a 1970s expansion team was Mike Bossy.

Gordie Howe had set a Red Wings record when he scored 49 goals in 1952–53. Frank Mahovlich tied the record in 1968–69. Who was the first Detroit player to score 50 goals in a season?

Ten players on five different teams had reached 100 points before a Montreal Canadiens player first reached the century mark. Who was he?

The 1971 Amateur Draft marks the only time that French Canadian players were selected 1–2–3. The Montreal Canadiens took Guy Lafleur with the first pick, followed by the Detroit Red Wings, who selected Marcel Dionne. Who was that year's third draft choice?

a) Jocelyn Guevremont   c) Jacques Richard

b) Rick Martin   d) Michel Larocque

Mickey Redmond scored 52 goals for Detroit in 1972–73, then scored 51 the next season. At the time, he joined Phil Esposito and Bobby Hull as the only players in the NHL to have more than one 50-goal season.

Guy Lafleur became the first Canadiens player to hit the 100-point plateau with a goal on March 7, 1975. Pete Mahovlich cracked 100 two days later. Lafleur and Mahovlich finished the season with 119 and 117 points respectively, trailing only Bobby Orr (135), Phil Esposito (127), and Marcel Dionne (121) in the scoring race. Lafleur won the first of his three straight scoring titles the following year.

The Vancouver Canucks chose Jocelyn Guevremont third overall in 1971. He'd been an all-star with the Montreal Junior Canadiens team that won the Memorial Cup in 1969 and 1970. Martin also played with that team (as did Gilbert Perreault) and was selected fifth overall in 1971. Jacques Richard went to the Atlanta Flames with the second pick in 1972. Michel Larocque was selected sixth overall by the Canadiens in 1972.

The Amateur Draft was renamed the Entry Draft in 1979 because formerly underage professional players from the WHA were made available to NHL teams. Put the following ex-WHA players in order of their selection in the 1979 NHL Entry Draft, starting with the highest pick:

a) Mark Messier   c) Mike Gartner

b) Rob Ramage   d) Michel Goulet

Match the following players to the team that selected them first overall in the draft and to the year in which they were chosen:

1) Bobby Smith   a) Washington   1972

2) Greg Joly   b) New York Islanders   1974

3) Dale McCourt   c) Minnesota   1975

4) Billy Harris   d) Philadelphia   1977

5) Mel Bridgman   e) Detroit   1978

b) Ramage was taken first overall by the Colorado Rockies after a season with the Birmingham Bulls. He'd been a junior star with the London Knights.

c) Gartner was taken fourth overall by the Washington Capitals after one season with the Cincinnati Stingers. He'd played junior hockey with the Niagara Falls Flyers.

d) Goulet was also a member of the Birmingham Bulls for a season before being selected 20th overall by the Quebec Nordiques. He'd played junior with the Quebec Remparts.

a) Messier split one WHA season with the Indianapolis Racers and the Cincinnati Stingers before being selected in the third round, 48th overall, by the Edmonton Oilers. He'd entered the WHA out of Tier-II junior hockey in Alberta.

Other first-round 1979 draft choices who'd played in the WHA were: Rick Vaive (Birmingham; Vancouver-5th) and Craig Hartsburg (Birmingham; Minnesota-6th).

1-c, 1978: Smith went on to win the Calder Trophy with the North Stars in 1978–79.

2-a, 1974: Joly was Washington's first-ever draft choice.

3-e, 1977: McCourt jumped right onto the Detroit roster and had 33 goals in 1977–78.

4-b, 1972: Harris was the Islanders' first-ever draft choice.

5-d, 1975: Bridgman was acquired with a pick obtained from the Capitals.

In addition to Bobby Orr, who else scored the Stanley Cup–winning goal in overtime during the 1970s?

a) Mike Bossy   c) Henri Richard

b) Guy Lafleur   d) Jacques Lemaire

When Bobby Hull jumped to the WHA with the Winnipeg Jets for the league's inaugural season of 1972–73, his 604 career goals ranked him second in NHL history behind Gordie Howe. His 1,153 points ranked fourth. Who was between Howe and Hull on the NHL's all-time scoring list?

What WHA team drafted Mark and Marty Howe, then signed their father, Gordie, and brought him out of a two-year retirement?

Jacques Lemaire took a pass from Guy Lafleur and fired the puck past Gerry Cheevers at 4:32 of overtime to give Montreal a 2–1 win over Boston and a four-game sweep of the 1977 Stanley Cup finals. At the time, Lemaire joined Maurice Richard (three) and Don Raleigh (two) as the only players in NHL history to score more than one overtime goal in the Stanley Cup finals. Lemaire's previous goal had come in game one back in 1968. John LeClair later scored two overtime goals in the 1993 finals.

Jean Beliveau, who, like Gordie Howe, had retired after the 1970–71 season, was second in NHL history with 1,219 points (507 goals, 712 assists). Alex Delvecchio, who was still active, had 1,205 (437, 768). Howe was well out in front with 786 goals and 1,023 assists for 1,809 points.

The three Howes joined the Houston Aeros for the WHA's second season of 1973–74. All three were signed as free agents by the New England Whalers in 1977–78 and were still playing together when the Whalers entered the NHL as Hartford in 1979–80.

Two different men coached the Boston Bruins to Stanley Cup titles in the 1970s. Two different coaches were also responsible for Montreal's six Stanley Cup victories, yet only one man was able to coach two different teams to the Stanley Cup finals during the decade. Name the five men involved.

The WHA had 12 teams when it first opened for business. Which one of these Canadian teams was not one of the league's original franchises?

a) Edmonton Oilers

b) Ottawa Nationals

c) Toronto Toros

d) Quebec Nordiques

Which one of these American teams was not an original WHA franchise?

a) Philadelphia Blazers

b) Phoenix Roadrunners

c) Los Angeles Sharks

d) Chicago Cougars

Harry Sinden coached Boston to victory in 1970, but then left the team to go into private business. (He would return in 1972–73.) Tom Johnson was behind the bench when the Bruins beat the Rangers in 1972. Al MacNeil coached the Canadiens to victory in 1971, while Scotty Bowman was behind the bench in 1973, 1976, 1977, 1978, and 1979. The one man who coached two different teams to the finals was Fred Shero. He led Philadelphia to the finals in 1974, 1975, and 1976 and the Rangers to the finals in 1979.

c: The Toros did not join the WHA until the second season of 1973–74. They replaced the league's Ottawa franchise. Winnipeg, Quebec, and Edmonton were all original WHA clubs, though Edmonton was known as the Alberta Oilers in 1972–73. In 1974–75 and 1975–76, the WHA had a Canadian Division made up of Quebec, Winnipeg, Toronto, Edmonton, and the Vancouver Blazers/Calgary Cowboys.

b: The Phoenix Roadrunners did not enter the WHA until the third season of 1974–75. The league's original eight American franchises were New England, Houston, Philadelphia, Los Angeles, Chicago, the Cleveland Crusaders, the New York Raiders, and the Minnesota Fighting Saints.

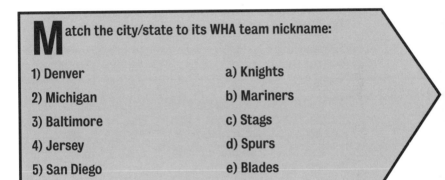

Match the city/state to its WHA team nickname:

1) Denver   a) Knights

2) Michigan   b) Mariners

3) Baltimore   c) Stags

4) Jersey   d) Spurs

5) San Diego   e) Blades

The biggest trade of the 1970s took place between the New York Rangers and Boston Bruins on November 7, 1975. Five players were involved. Can you name them all?

1-d: The Denver Spurs played their first game on October 10, 1975, but drew poorly and became the Ottawa Civics in midseason (January 2, 1976). After losing six of seven games in Ottawa, the club folded on January 17.

2-c: The Los Angeles Sharks transferred to Detroit shortly after the 1973–74 season and opened the 1974–75 campaign as the Michigan Stags.

3-e: When the Michigan Stags folded in midseason (January 18, 1975), the WHA used their players to form the Baltimore Blades. The Blades folded after the season.

4-a: The New York Raiders had hoped to set up shop on Long Island in 1972–73, but when the NHL placed a new expansion team there, the Raiders tried to share Madison Square Garden with the Rangers. The Raiders were renamed the Golden Blades by new ownership in 1973–74, but the WHA bailed out of the Big Apple early in the season. The team was moved to the Cherry Hill Arena in Cherry Hill, New Jersey, and finished out the season as the Jersey Knights.

5-b: New ownership of the Jersey Knights moved the team to San Diego for the 1974–75 season. The Mariners lasted three seasons, but when plans to move the team to Florida fell through, the club folded well before the 1977–78 season.

The Bruins dealt Phil Esposito and Carol Vadnais to New York for Jean Ratelle, Brad Park, and Joe Zanussi.

Originally known simply as the World Trophy, by what name would the WHA's championship award become known?

Match the player to his accomplishment in the WHA:

1) Bobby Hull   a) first Toronto pro player to score 50 goals

2) Tom Simpson   b) set a pro hockey record with 77 goals

3) Gordie Howe   c) set a pro hockey record with 106 assists

4) Marc Tardif   d) set a pro hockey record with 154 points

5) Andre Lacroix   e) played a record 78 WHA playoff games

Champions of the WHA were crowned with the AVCO Cup, named for the AVCO Financial Services Corporation. New England won the first championship in 1972–73. Houston won it in 1974 and 1975, Winnipeg won it in 1976, 1978, and 1979, and Quebec won it in 1977.

1-b: Hull's 77 goals for the Winnipeg Jets in 1974–75 gave him one more than Phil Esposito's NHL record of 76.

2-a: "Shotgun" Tom Simpson scored 52 goals for the Toros in 1974–75. Czechoslovakian defector Vaclav Nedomansky scored 56 for Toronto the following year. At the time, no Maple Leafs player had ever scored 50 goals.

3-e: Gordie Howe's 78 career playoff games were the most in WHA history, ranking him just ahead of sons Marty (75) and Mark (74). Howe's 508 points in six WHA seasons rank him sixth in league scoring.

4-d: Tardif's 154 points for Quebec in 1977–78 broke his own league record of 148 and surpassed Phil Esposito's NHL mark of 152. Tardif is the WHA's all-time leader with 316 goals, 13 more than Bobby Hull.

5-c: Lacroix's 106 assists for San Diego in 1974–75 were four more than the NHL record of 102 assists held by Bobby Orr. Lacroix is the WHA's all-time leader in games played (551), assists (547), and points (798).

Chapter 9

Hockey in the 1980s

Though he had finished third in scoring in the WHA the season before, few people expected much from Wayne Gretzky when he entered the NHL as an 18-year-old in 1979–80. All he did was tie Marcel Dionne for the league lead in scoring with 137 points, then the third-highest single-season total in NHL history. In his second season, Gretzky broke Phil Esposito's record of 152 points with 55 goals and 109 assists. In 1981–82, he smashed another Esposito record with 92 goals and collected 120 assists for an astounding 212 points. No player had ever set so many records at such an astonishing rate as the player who became known as the "Great One."

Gretzky and the Edmonton Oilers led an offensive revolution

in the 1980s as more European players and an improving U.S. college system put more talented performers into the NHL than ever before. With stars like Mark Messier, Glenn Anderson, Paul Coffey, and Jari Kurri, the Oilers played a blend of European and North American styles. They became the first team in NHL history to score 400 goals in 1981–82, a feat they accomplished for five straight years. In 1983–84, the Oilers scored a record 446 goals. That same year, Edmonton ended the New York Islanders' run of four straight Stanley Cup titles and launched a dynasty of their own.

Hockey fans of the 1980s were most fortunate indeed. Not only did they have number 99 to watch, but number 66 as well. Mario Lemieux entered the NHL with a 100-point season in 1984–85 and ended Wayne Gretzky's seven-year hold on the Art Ross Trophy with the first of back-to-back scoring titles in 1987–88. By the 1988–89 season, Wayne Gretzky was in Los Angeles bringing new fans to the game from all across the United States.

Because of his season in the WHA, Wayne Gretzky was not considered a rookie when he entered the NHL in 1979–80. Who was the top rookie scorer that season and who was the winner of the Calder Trophy?

Wayne Gretzky broke Bobby Orr's single-season assist record with 109 in 1980–81 when he also set a new scoring record with 164 points. Who finished second behind Gretzky in scoring that season?

a) Mike Bossy

b) Marcel Dionne

c) Bryan Trottier

d) Kent Nilsson

Who was the goaltender that surrendered Wayne Gretzky's record-breaking 77th goal of the season in 1981–82?

Mike Foligno led all rookie scorers with 71 points (36 goals, 35 assists) for the Detroit Red Wings in 1979–80. He finished as the runner-up in voting for the Calder Trophy, which was won by Ray Bourque of the Boston Bruins.

b: Marcel Dionne, who had tied Gretzky for the scoring lead with 137 points but won the Art Ross Trophy in 1979–80, was runner-up behind Gretzky with 135 points in 1980–81. Kent Nilsson was third with 131 points. Mike Bossy was fourth with 119, and Trottier finished tied for tenth with 103. The 1980–81 season marked the first time in history that every scorer in the top 10 had more than 100 points.

After scoring 50 goals in just 39 games in 1981–82, Wayne Gretzky tied Phil Esposito's single-season record of 76 goals by his 63rd game. One game later, on February 24, 1982, Gretzky had been shut out into the third period until he stole the puck at the Buffalo blueline and slipped a shot between Don Edward's legs. Gretzky went on to score two more goals and finished the night with 79.

One year before Wayne Gretzky shattered the mark with 50 goals in 39 games, Mike Bossy had matched Maurice Richard when he scored 50 goals in 50 games in 1980–81. Name the player who scored 49 goals in 50 games that year and notched his 50th in game number 51.

Three different defensemen won the Norris Trophy in back-to-back seasons over a six-year span during the 1980s. Name them.

Can you name the four other defensemen who won the Norris Trophy between 1979–80 and 1988–89?

Charlie Simmer scored 56 goals in 1979–80 before suffering a season-ending injury after playing just 64 games. Red hot again in 1980–81, he had 46 goals through 49 games. Mike Bossy had 48. Both would play their 50th game on Saturday, January 24, 1981, but Simmer had a chance to match the record first because he played an afternoon game in Boston. He scored three goals that day (though his third came with only one second left) and fell just short. Bossy scored two that night against Quebec. Simmer scored his 50th against the Nordiques two nights later and was at 56 goals again when his season was shortened by another serious injury, this time in his 65th game.

Rod Langway of Washington was named the NHL's best defenseman in 1982–83 and 1983–84. Edmonton's Paul Coffey won the Norris in 1984–85 and 1985–86. Boston's Ray Bourque took the honors in 1986–87 and 1987–88.

Montreal's Larry Robinson won the Norris in 1979–80, followed by Randy Carlyle of Pittsburgh the next year. Chicago's Doug Wilson won the award in 1981–82, and Chris Chelios of the Canadiens earned the Norris in 1988–89.

Put the following events in chronological order, starting with the earliest:

a) Mario Lemieux wins the Calder Trophy

b) Wayne Gretzky records 163 assists

c) Ron Hextall scores a goal

d) Grant Fuhr wins his first game

Match the player to his accomplishment during the 1980s:

1) Bernie Federko   a) at least 50 assists for 10 straight seasons

2) Anton Stastny   b) first American to score five goals in a game

3) Mark Pavelich   c) first to score a goal in all four periods of a game

4) Dino Ciccarelli   d) had a record eight points in one road game

5) Bernie Nicholls   e) fastest 20 goals from the start of a season

d) Grant Fuhr got his first victory on October 21, 1981. Edmonton beat Hartford 5–2.

a) Mario Lemieux was the rookie of the year in 1984–85.

b) Wayne Gretzky broke his own records with 163 assists and 215 points in 1985–86.

c) Ron Hextall fired the puck into an open net for the first time on December 8, 1987. He would do it again on April 11, 1989. The first goalie to be credited with scoring a goal was Billy Smith of the New York Islanders on November 28, 1979. He was the last player to touch the puck before Rob Ramage of the Colorado Rockies put it in his own net.

1-a: Federko was the first player in NHL history to have at least 50 assists for 10 straight seasons, a streak that stretched from 1978–79 to 1987–88.

2-d: Both Peter and Anton Stastny had eight points in one road game as Quebec beat the Capitals 11–7 in Washington on February 22, 1981.

3-b: Pavelich, a member of the 1980 U.S. Olympic team, scored five goals for the New York Rangers in an 11–3 win over Hartford on February 23, 1983.

4-e: Ciccarelli had 20 goals in just 15 games to start the 1986–87 season. He scored 52 goals that year.

5-c: Nicholls scored in the first, second, and third periods, then netted the game winner in overtime when Los Angeles beat Quebec 5–4 on November 13, 1984.

Six different players scored their 500th career goal during the 1980s. The first to do it was Marcel Dionne on December 14, 1982. The last was Lanny McDonald on March 21, 1989. Put the other four players in order of when they scored their 500th goal, starting with the earliest:

a) Mike Bossy

c) Wayne Gretzky

b) Guy Lafleur

d) Gilbert Perreault

Who became the first European player to be selected first overall in the NHL Entry Draft in 1989?

Wayne Gretzky was just the 18th player in NHL history to reach the 1,000-point plateau when he did it on December 19, 1984. He reached the milestone in his 424th game, shattering the previous record of 720 games. Whose record did Gretzky break?

a) Phil Esposito

c) Guy Lafleur

b) Marcel Dionne

d) Mike Bossy

b) Guy Lafleur   December 20, 1983

a) Mike Bossy   January 2, 1986

d) Gilbert Perreault   March 9, 1986

c) Wayne Gretzky   November 22, 1986

The Quebec Nordiques made Mats Sundin the first pick in the 1989 draft. He spent one more year in the Swedish elite league before making his NHL debut in 1990–91. The 1989 draft was a good year for European talent, as Nicklas Lidstrom, Bobby Holik, Robert Reichel, Sergei Fedorov, and Pavel Bure were all selected.

c: Guy Lafleur had recorded his 1,000th point in his 720th game, which was 20 games faster than Marcel Dionne. Phil Esposito got his 1,000th point in 745 games. Mike Bossy reached the 1,000-point plateau a year after Gretzky, doing it in 656 games. Peter Stastny (682) and Mario Lemieux (513) are the only other players to reach 1,000 points in less than 700 games.

The Pittsburgh Penguins selected Mario Lemieux first overall in the 1984 NHL Entry Draft. Who was the second pick that year?

In his first NHL game on October 11, 1984, Mario Lemieux stole the puck from an opposing defenseman and scored his first NHL goal on his very first shot. Who was the defenseman?

The 1980–81 season marked the last time that the Vezina Trophy was presented to the goalies on the team with the best defensive record. Three Canadiens teammates shared the honor that year. Which of the following was <u>not</u> one of them?

a) Rick Wamsley

c) Denis Herron

b) Richard Sevigny

d) Michel Larocque

New Jersey selected Kirk Muller with the second choice in the draft. He had played junior hockey in Kingston and Guelph and was a member of the 1984 Canadian Olympic team prior to being picked by the Devils.

On his very first shift, Lemieux knocked the puck away from Ray Bourque, swooped in on Boston goaltender Pete Peeters and deked him for a goal. Still, the Bruins won the game 4–3.

a: Rick Wamsley played only five games for the Canadiens that year, and so was not eligible to share in the award with the three others. However, when the Jennings Trophy was introduced the following season, Wamsley shared that with Denis Herron. Larocque got his name on the Vezina in 1980–81 even though he was traded to Toronto during the season. (He had already played 28 games for Montreal.) Sevigny played 33 games and Herron 25.

Name the player who established a rookie scoring record (later broken by Teemu Selanne) when he recorded 109 points in 1980–81.

After the Jennings Trophy was introduced in 1981–82 and the Vezina became an award for the goalie adjudged to be the best at his position, eight different goaltenders won the Vezina Trophy in the next eight years. How many can you name?

What is the common link among these four players?

a) Bob Carpenter

b) Phil Housley

c) Brian Lawton

d) Tom Barrasso

Though Wayne Gretzky's single season in the WHA made him ineligible for any rookie records, Peter Stastny's five years in the Czechoslovakian elite league and in major international competition did not affect his rookie status. He had 39 goals and 70 assists for the Quebec Nordiques and won the Calder Trophy.

Billy Smith	Islanders	1981–82
Pete Peeters	Boston	1982–83
Tom Barrasso	Buffalo	1983–84
Pelle Lindbergh	Philadelphia	1984–85
John Vanbiesbrouck	New York Rangers	1985–86
Ron Hextall	Philadelphia	1986–87
Grant Fuhr	Edmonton	1987–88
Patrick Roy	Montreal	1988–89

All four of these players were Americans who were selected in the first round of the Entry Draft and jumped to the NHL directly out of high school. Lawton was the first American to be picked number one in the draft when the North Stars selected him in 1983. Tom Barrasso was selected fifth that year. Bobby Carpenter had been the third choice in 1981 and Phil Housley the sixth in 1982.

Who does not belong among this group of four players and why?

a) Dale Hawerchuk

b) Brian Bellows

c) Joe Murphy

d) Mike Modano

Who were the two players selected ahead of Denis Savard in the 1980 NHL Entry Draft?

Match the first overall draft choice to the junior team from which he was selected:

1) Wendel Clark

2) Dale Hawerchuk

3) Mario Lemieux

4) Mike Modano

5) Pierre Turgeon

a) Laval

b) Granby

c) Cornwall

d) Saskatoon

e) Prince Albert

b: Brian Bellows is the only one of the four who was not selected first overall in the NHL Entry Draft. He was selected second by the Minnesota North Stars, behind Gord Kluzak, in 1982. Dale Hawerchuk was chosen first by Winnipeg in 1981, Joe Murphy by Detroit in 1986 and Mike Modano by Minnesota in 1988.

Though Doug Wickenheiser of the Regina Pats was the top-rated prospect from the Western Hockey League, Montreal fans were shocked when the Canadiens opted for him over local favorite Denis Savard. The Winnipeg Jets then made Dave Babych the second pick before Chicago grabbed Savard with the third.

1-d: The Maple Leafs selected Clark from the Saskatoon Blades in 1985 and converted him from defense to left wing.

2-c: Hawerchuk led the Cornwall Royals to back-to-back Memorial Cup championships before being selected by Winnipeg in 1981.

3-a: Lemieux had 133 goals and 149 assists for 282 points in 70 games with the Laval Titan in 1983–84 before becoming the top pick in the Entry Draft.

4-e: Just the second American to be picked first overall in the Entry Draft, Modano spent three years playing junior hockey in Canada with the Prince Albert Raiders.

5-b: Turgeon spent two seasons with the Granby Bisons before the Buffalo Sabres selected him first overall in 1987.

Wayne Gretzky topped 200 points four times in the 1980s, and Mario Lemieux had 199 when he won the Art Ross Trophy in 1987–88. Between them, Gretzky and Lemieux had at least 164 points 10 times during the decade. Gretzky also had 149 points in 1987–88, while Lemieux had 141 in 1985–86. Match the following players to the next best scoring numbers put up during the 1980s:

1) Mike Bossy	a) 150
2) Peter Stastny	b) 147
3) Steve Yzerman	c) 139
4) Paul Coffey	d) 138
5) Bernie Nicholls	e) 155

The Islanders and the Oilers were the decade's most dominant teams, winning the Stanley Cup eight times between them. Name the only player to win the Stanley Cup with both the Islanders and Edmonton during the 1980s.

1-b: Bossy had 147 points (64 goals, 83 assists) in 1981–82. He finished second in scoring behind Gretzky's 212 that year.

2-c: Stastny had 139 points (46 goals, 93 assists) in 1981–82 to finish third in scoring behind Gretzky and Bossy.

3-e: Yzerman's 155 points in 1988–89 are the most ever scored by a player other than Gretzky and Lemieux.

4-d: Coffey had 138 points in 1985–86 to finish third behind Gretzky (215) and Lemieux (141). Coffey's 48 goals that year broke Bobby Orr's record of 46 by a defenseman, but his points total was one behind Orr's record set in 1970–71.

5-a: Nicholls had 150 points (70 goals, 80 assists) in 1988–89, but finished fourth in scoring behind Lemieux (199), Gretzky (168), and Yzerman (155).

Billy Carroll won the Stanley Cup with the Islanders as a rookie in 1980–81. He won it again in 1982 and 1983, then won with the Oilers in 1985. He was traded to Detroit the following season.

Who did the Edmonton Oilers beat to win the franchise's first NHL playoff series?

Name the Hockey Hall of Famer who won the Stanley Cup for the first time in the final game of his 16-year career?

On August 9, 1988, Wayne Gretzky and two other players were dealt to the Los Angeles Kings for two players, three future first-round draft choices, and millions of dollars. Name the four other players who were part of the trade.

Ice Q and As

The Oilers were the 16th and final team to qualify for the playoffs in 1979–80, and were swept by the first-overall Philadelphia Flyers in a best-of-five first-round series. Edmonton was seeded 14th in 1980–81 and were considered huge underdogs against the Montreal Canadiens. Instead, they swept the series in three and then pushed the defending champion Islanders to six games before bowing out in round two.

In his final season of 1988–89, Lanny McDonald scored his 500th goal, collected his 1,000th point, and scored the insurance goal as the Calgary Flames beat the Canadiens 4–2 in game six to win the Stanley Cup.

In addition to Wayne Gretzky, the Oilers sent Mike Krushelnyski and Marty McSorley to the Kings. The two players Los Angeles gave up were Jimmy Carson and Martin Gelinas.

Chapter 10

Hockey in the 1990s

The NHL truly became an international sports league in the 1990s, as the fall of Communism made players readily available from former Eastern Bloc nations. Indeed, by the end of the decade, a total of 38 non–North American countries—and 38 of 50 U.S. states—had produced at least one NHL hockey player. So had 885 Canadian cities or towns. The abundant supply of available talent helped fuel an expansion of the NHL from 21 teams to 30. Salaries also skyrocketed. The average annual income was $108,000 when Wayne Gretzky entered the NHL in 1979–80. By his final season of 1998–99, the average had climbed above $1 million.

After ten years of franchise stability, the NHL added its 22nd team when the San Jose Sharks played their first season in 1991–92. The Ottawa Senators and Tampa Bay Lightning came on board the following year, followed by the Florida Panthers and the Mighty Ducks of Anaheim in 1993–94. In 1995, the NHL granted future franchises to Nashville, Atlanta, Columbus, and Minnesota.

Previous expansions had all produced an explosion of offense, but defense came to the forefront in the new NHL. In 1992–93, only two goaltenders had posted a goals-against average below 3.00, but in 1993–94, 19 goalies broke that barrier. The 1995 Stanley Cup finals introduced a new term to North American hockey audiences, as the New Jersey Devils shut down the Detroit Red Wings with a tactic known as the "Neutral Zone Trap."

Defensive hockey brought goaltenders to the forefront in the 1990s, and none more so than Dominik Hasek who became just the fifth goalie in NHL history to win the Hart Trophy in 1996–97, then the first to win it back-to-back in 1997–98. In 1999–2000, Chris Pronger became the first defenseman to win the Hart Trophy since Bobby Orr in 1972.

When Dominik Hasek posted a 1.95 goals-against average in 1993–94, he became the first goalie in 20 seasons with an average below 2.00. Who had been the last goalie to do it?

a) Ken Dryden   c) Tony Esposito

b) Bernie Parent   d) Jacques Plante

The members of the Soviets' famed KLM Line were all allowed to enter the NHL in 1989–90. Name the three players and the NHL teams that they joined.

Who became the first goaltender since Ken Dryden in 1976–77 to reach double digits in shutouts when he recorded 10 in 1996–97?

a) Ed Belfour   c) Martin Brodeur

b) Dominik Hasek   d) Olaf Kolzig

b: Bernie Parent had a 1.89 goals-against average for the Philadelphia Flyers in 1973–74.

Vladimir Krutov and Igor Larionov joined the Vancouver Canucks. Krutov was a bust and returned to Europe the following season, but Larionov would prove to be a valuable player. He played three seasons in Vancouver, then joined San Jose, who later sent him to Detroit. He played on two Stanley Cup winners with the Red Wings and was still active through the 2000–01 season. Sergei Makarov played seven seasons in the NHL. Despite the fact that he was a seasoned international veteran, he won the Calder Trophy with the Calgary Flames in 1989–90. After that, the rules were changed to say that a player had to be under 26 years old to qualify as rookie of the year.

Not only did Martin Brodeur have 10 shutouts in 1996–97, he had 10 again in 1997–98 to become the first to reach double digits in back-to-back years since Bernie Parent had 12 in both 1973–74 and 1974–75.

In addition to his two Hart Trophy wins, Dominik Hasek won the Vezina Trophy five times in the 1990s. Match the following trophies to the first European-trained player to win it:

1) Art Ross Trophy   a) Mats Naslund

2) Hart Trophy   b) Peter Stastny

3) Lady Byng Trophy   c) Pelle Lindbergh

4) Vezina Trophy   d) Jaromir Jagr

5) Calder Trophy   e) Sergei Fedorov

Four NHL teams were relocated in the 1990s. The Minnesota North Stars became the Dallas Stars in 1993–94, the Quebec Nordiques became the Colorado Avalanche in 1995–96, the Winnipeg Jets became the Phoenix Coyotes in 1996–97, and the Hartford Whalers became the Carolina Hurricanes in 1997–98. What became of the following four teams?

a) Oakland Seals   c) Colorado Rockies

b) Kansas City Scouts   d) Atlanta Flames

1-d: Jagr first won the Art Ross Trophy as the league's top scorer in 1994–95.

2-e: Fedorov won the Hart Trophy as the NHL MVP in 1993–94. That same season he was the first European player to win the Selke Trophy as best defensive forward.

3-a: Naslund won the Lady Byng Trophy for sportsmanlike conduct in 1987–88.

4-c: Lindbergh won the Vezina Trophy as the NHL's top goaltender in 1984–85.

5-b: Stastny won the Calder Trophy as rookie of the year in 1980–81.

a) The Oakland Seals, who were also known as the California Seals and the California Golden Seals, became the Cleveland Barons in 1976–77. After two more disappointing seasons, the franchise merged with the Minnesota North Stars in 1978–79, reducing the NHL from 18 to 17 teams.

b) After just two seasons in Kansas City, the Scouts became the Colorado Rockies in 1976–77.

c) After six seasons in Colorado, the Rockies became the New Jersey Devils in 1982–83.

d) After eight seasons in Atlanta, the Flames moved to Calgary in 1980–81.

Six of the 10 Calder Trophy winners during the 1990s were European players. How many of them can you name?

Which of these players was <u>not</u> chosen first overall by the Ottawa Senators:

a) Alexei Yashin

c) Bryan Berard

b) Alexandre Daigle

d) Chris Phillips

Four other players were involved in the deal that sent Patrick Roy from Montreal to Colorado on December 6, 1995. Can you name them?

Sergei Makarov	Russia	1990
Pavel Bure	Russia	1992
Teemu Selanne	Finland	1993
Peter Forsberg	Sweden	1995
Daniel Alfredsson	Sweden	1996
Sergei Samsonov	Russia	1998

Ed Belfour (1991) and Martin Brodeur (1994) were Canadian rookies of the year. Bryan Berard (1997) and Chris Drury (1999) were Americans.

a: Alexei Yashin was the second player taken in the 1992 Entry Draft. Tampa Bay had the first pick that year and chose Roman Hamrlik. Alexandre Daigle went first overall in 1993, Bryan Berard in 1995, and Chris Phillips in 1996. Berard refused to sign with the Senators and was later traded to the New York Islanders for Wade Redden, who had been picked second overall behind Berard.

Mike Keane accompanied Patrick Roy to Colorado. The Canadiens received Andrei Kovalenko, Martin Rucinsky, and Jocelyn Thibault in return.

Match the player to the single–season record he set or tied during the 1990s:

1) Brett Hull   a) most goals in one period

2) Luc Robitaille b) most goals by a rightwinger

3) Peter Bondra c) most points by a rightwinger

4) Jaromir Jagr   d) most goal by a leftwinger

5) Joe Juneau   e) most assists by a leftwinger

Match the team to the record it set during the 1990s:

1) Toronto Maple Leafs a) most wins in a season

2) Montreal Canadiens b) most consecutive wins

3) Pittsburgh Penguins c) most consecutive wins to open the season

4) Detroit Red Wings d) most road wins in one season

5) New Jersey Devils e) most playoff overtime wins

1-b: Hull's 86 goals in 1990–91 are the third most in NHL history and the most ever by a rightwinger.

2-d: Robitaille's 63 goals in 1992–93 broke Steve Shutt's record of 60 goals by a leftwinger. His 125 points that year are also a record for leftwingers.

3-a: Bondra became the 10th player in NHL history to score four goals in one period (the first) on February 5, 1994.

4-c: Jagr's 149 points in 1995–96 broke Mike Bossy's record of 147 points by a rightwinger. His 87 assists that year broke Bossy's record of 83.

5-e: Juneau's 70 assists in 1992–93 are the most ever by a leftwinger and tied Peter Statsny's record for the most assists by a rookie.

1-c: The Leafs opened the 1993–94 season with 10 straight wins, breaking the record of eight shared by the 1934–35 Leafs and the 1975–76 Sabres.

2-e: The Canadiens won 10 games in overtime en route to the 1993 Stanley Cup. No other team has ever won more than six overtime games.

3-b: The Penguins won 17 in a row from March 9 to April 10, 1993, breaking the record of 15 in a row set by the Islanders during the 1981–82 season.

4-a: The Red Wings went 62–13–7 in 1995–96, breaking the Canadiens record of 60 wins in 1976–77, but falling one point short (132–131) of Montreal's record for most points in a season.

5-d: The Devils went 28–10–3 in 41 games on the road in 1998–99, breaking the Canadiens record of 27 wins set twice during 80-game seasons in the 1970s.

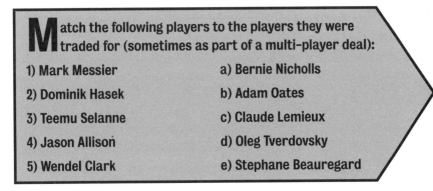

Match the following players to the players they were traded for (sometimes as part of a multi-player deal):

1) Mark Messier
2) Dominik Hasek
3) Teemu Selanne
4) Jason Allison
5) Wendel Clark

a) Bernie Nicholls
b) Adam Oates
c) Claude Lemieux
d) Oleg Tverdovsky
e) Stephane Beauregard

The 1991 Stanley Cup final between Pittsburgh and Minnesota marked the first time since 1981 that a Canadian team was not playing for the championship. The series also marked the first time that something had happened since 1934. What was it?

1-a: The Oilers traded Messier (and future considerations) to the Rangers for Bernie Nicholls, Steven Rice, and Louie DeBrusk on October 4, 1991.

2-e: The Sabres obtained Hasek from Chicago for Beauregard and a fourth-round draft choice on August 7, 1992. The Blackhawks used the pick to obtain Eric Daze.

3-d: Anaheim got Selanne, Marc Chouinard, and a fourth-round draft choice from the Jets for Tverdovsky, Chad Kilger, and a third-round pick on February 7, 1996.

4-b: Allison, Anson Carter, and Jim Carey were traded from Washington to Boston for Adam Oates, Rick Tocchet, and Bill Ranford on March 1, 1997.

5-c: Clark was with Quebec when the team moved to Colorado, but the Avalanche sent him to the Islanders for Claude Lemieux on October 3, 1995. Lemieux had been traded from the Devils to the Islanders for Steve Thomas earlier that day.

The series between the Penguins and North Stars marked the first time since the Red Wings faced the Blackhawks in 1934 that neither finalist had ever won the Stanley Cup. This would occur twice more in the '90s: when Colorado faced Florida in 1996 and when Dallas played Buffalo in 1999. Colorado's win, following on the heels of New Jersey's first victory in 1995, marked the first time since the Rangers and Bruins in 1928 and 1929 that first-time champions had won the Cup in back-to-back years.

Tom Barrasso was in goal for 12 of Pittsburgh's 16 playoff victories when they first won the Stanley Cup in 1991. Who was in net for the other four victories?

a) Frank Pietrangelo   c) Steve Guenette

b) Ken Wregget   d) Wendell Young

Four players all scored their 500th goal during the 1995–96 season. Name them.

Put the following players in order of goals scored during their rookie season, starting with the fewest:

a) Tony Amonte   c) Eric Lindros

b) Pavel Bure   d) Teemu Selanne

a: Frank Pietrangelo had a 4–1 record in five playoff games for the Penguins in 1991. His biggest victory came with a 4–0 shutout of New Jersey in game seven of the opening round. Wendell Young was a member of both Pittsburgh Cup winners, but saw no action in the playoffs in either year. Ken Wregget didn't come on board until late in the 1991–92 season. Guenette had been traded by the Penguins back in 1989.

Mario Lemieux reached the milestone on October 26, 1995. Mark Messier was next on November 6. Steve Yzerman scored number 500 on January 17, 1996. Dale Hawerchuk got his on January 31.

b) Bure had 34 goals and 26 assists for 60 points in 65 games as a rookie with the Vancouver Canucks in 1991–92. He had 60 goals in each of the next two years.

a) Amonte had 35 goals and 69 points for the New York Rangers to lead all rookie scorers in 1991–92. He was third behind Pavel Bure and Nicklas Lidstrom in voting for the Calder Trophy.

c) Lindros had 41 goals in just 61 games as a rookie with the Flyers in 1992–93. It was the second highest rookie total that year behind Teemu Selanne.

d) Selanne's 76 goals with the Winnipeg Jets in 1992–93 shattered Mike Bossy's rookie record of 53 goals. With 56 assists that season, the "Finnish Flash" also smashed Peter Stastny's rookie record of 109 points.

Eric Lindros was chosen first overall by the Quebec Nordiques in 1991 even though he had already warned them that he would not sign. Match the following players to the team that originally drafted them:

1) Peter Forsberg   a) Montreal Canadiens

2) Chris Pronger   b) Philadelphia Flyers

3) Valeri Bure   c) Hartford Whalers

4) Sandis Ozolinsh   d) Undrafted

5) Curtis Joseph   e) San Jose Sharks

Chris McRae was a player who relied more on his powerful punch than his soft hands. He played only 21 games in the NHL and scored his only goal for the Detroit Red Wings during the 1989–90 season. Yet McRae's lone tally is unique in all of hockey history. Do you know why?

1-b: Forsberg was selected sixth overall by the Flyers in 1991, but was traded to Quebec one year later as part of the package that brought Lindros to Philadelphia. Forsberg broke in with Quebec in 1994–95, then moved to Colorado when the Nordiques relocated after the season.

2-c: Pronger was picked second overall behind Alexandre Daigle by the Hartford Whalers in 1993. He was traded to St. Louis before the 1995–96 season.

3-a: Bure was selected 33rd overall by Montreal in 1992. He was in his fourth season with the Canadiens when he and a draft choice were sent to Calgary for Jonas Hoglund and Zarley Zalapski.

4-e: Ozolinsh was selected by San Jose with the 30th pick in the 1991 Entry Draft. He broke in with the Sharks in 1992–93, but was traded to Colorado for Owen Nolan during the 1995–96 season. He was dealt to Carolina after the 1999–2000 season.

5-d: Curtis Joseph was never drafted. St. Louis signed him as a free agent in 1989. He spent six seasons with the Blues before being dealt to Edmonton. He signed with Toronto as a free agent prior to the 1998–99 season.

Chris McRae is the only player in NHL history to score a goal on his only career shot on goal! His lifetime shooting percentage is 1.000.

The last remaining player to play in the NHL without a helmet announced his retirement on April 29, 1997. Name him.

Wayne Gretzky announced his retirement on April 16, 1999, and played his final game two days later. His Rangers lost 2–1 on an overtime goal by Jaromir Jagr, but Gretzky had at least managed to set up his team's lone goal. Who scored the last goal ever assisted by Wayne Gretzky?

Name the cities that have been home to more than one franchise over the course of NHL history.

Craig MacTavish broke into the NHL with Boston in 1979–80, but he had already signed a contract prior to June 1, 1979—the date after which all newly signed players would have to wear protective headgear. By the 1995–96 season, MacTavish was the last bareheaded player left in the NHL.

A goal by Brian Leetch gave Wayne Gretzky the 1,963rd assist of his career. Since recording his 1,851st assist on October 26, 1997, Gretzky had more assists than any other player has ever had points.

Atlanta: Flames and Thrashers

Minnesota: North Stars and Wild

Montreal: Canadiens, Maroons, and Wanderers

New York: Rangers, Islanders, and Americans

Ottawa: two different Senators franchises

Philadelphia: Quakers and Flyers

Pittsburgh: Pirates and Penguins

St. Louis: Eagles and Blues

Toronto has had the Leafs, St. Pats, and Arenas, and Detroit has had the Cougars, Falcons, and Red Wings, but those have all just been different names for the same franchise.

What is the common link among these four players?

a) Mats Sundin

b) Peter Bondra

c) Mike Ricci

d) Alexei Zhamnov

Name the player who finished as the runner-up behind Peter Forsberg in Calder Trophy voting in 1994–95, then won the Vezina Trophy in 1995–96.

Wayne Gretzky scored the final goal of his career on March 29, 1999. Who was the goalie he scored on and what was significant about the goal?

All four of them scored five goals in a game during the 1990s. Sundin did it for Quebec in a 10–4 win over Hartford on March 5, 1992. Bondra did it for Washington in a 6–3 win over Tampa Bay on February 5, 1994. Ricci did it for Quebec in an 8–2 win over San Jose on February 17, 1994. Zhamnov did it for Winnipeg on April 1, 1995. Two other players had five-goal games during the 1990s. Sergei Fedorov scored all five goals for the Red Wings in a 5–4 win over Washington on December 26, 1996. Mario Lemieux had pair of five-goal games during the decade.

Jim Carey of the Washington Capitals was not called up from the minors until March 1, 1995, but he made up for lost time by going undefeated in his first seven games (6–0–1). He finished the season with an 18–6–3 record, four shutouts, and a 2.13 goals-against average. The next year, Carey led the league with nine shutouts, ranked second with 35 wins and third with a 2.23 average. However, he was sent to Boston in a blockbuster deal the following year and was back in the minors by 1997–98.

When Wayne Gretzky slipped the puck past Wade Flaherty of the New York Islanders, it gave him 1,072 goals in his professional career (NHL and WHA, regular season and playoffs combined)—one more than Gordie Howe. Gretzky scored 894 regular-season NHL goals, 122 NHL playoff goals, 46 WHA regular-season goals, and 10 WHA playoff goals. Gordie Howe had 801 and 68 plus 174 and 48.

Put the following events in order, starting with the earliest:

a) NHL realigns into six divisions

b) USA wins World Cup of Hockey

c) Gretzky traded to St. Louis

d) Lemieux takes season off

On March 23, 1994, Wayne Gretzky scored his 802nd goal to surpass Gordie Howe as the NHL's all-time goal-scoring leader. He would retire with 894 goals. A total of 143 different players had assists on Gretzky goals. Rank the following players in order of the number of times they helped set up the "Great One":

a) Mark Messier

b) Jari Kurri

c) Paul Coffey

d) Glenn Anderson

d) Mario Lemieux sat out the entire 1994–95 to recuperate from back injuries and his battle with cancer. He missed only a shortened 48-game campaign, as a lockout delayed the start of the season by 103 days.

c) While Lemieux returned to score 69 goals in 70 games in 1995–96, Wayne Gretzky and the Kings were slumping. The "Great One" was dealt to St. Louis on February 27, 1996. He signed with the Rangers as a free agent after the season.

b) The World Cup of Hockey, a successor to the Canada Cup, was held in August and September of 1996. Team Canada beat the USA in game one of the final, but the Americans rebounded to win the best-of-three series.

a) The NHL, which had switched to geographical division names in 1993–94, realigned into six divisions for the 1998–99 season.

b) Kurri, 196 assists

c) Coffey, 116 assists

a) Messier, 68 assists

d) Anderson, 63 assists

Chapter 11

Great Goalies

Whereas once they were barefaced men lugging 40 pounds of sweaty equipment, today's NHL goaltenders are probably the best-protected men in all of sports. Lightweight materials and face-hugging masks have helped the current crop of men in the nets post some of the best defensive numbers since before the days of the forward pass. Still, it takes a special breed of person to be willing to throw himself in front of a black block of rubber that can travel like a speeding bullet.

Well protected or not, the goalie has always been the last line of defense. All the other players on the ice can afford to make a mistake without everyone noticing, but when the goalie messes up, red lights flash, foghorns blare, rock music pounds, and another number goes up on the scoreboard. "How would you like it," Jacques Plante used to say, "if I followed you to work and booed every time you made a mistake?"

Plante was part of a long line of legendary goaltenders in Montreal. It all began with Georges Vezina, who joined the Canadiens for their second season of 1910–11. Over the next 15 years, Vezina never missed a game—regular-season or playoffs—in a streak that reached 367 before he was sidelined by an illness (tuberculosis) that would soon claim his life.

Eighty-five years after Vezina's debut, a rookie named Patrick Roy led the Canadiens to the Stanley Cup. Roy's heroics in Montreal, combined with his innovative style of playing low to the ice—a style made possible by the improvements in equipment—are generally credited with inspiring the new generation of goaltenders who are dominating the game today. Roy became the winningest goalie in NHL history when he recorded his 448th victory on October 17, 2000.

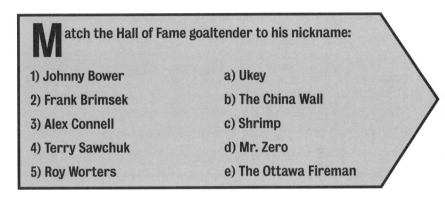

Match the Hall of Fame goaltender to his nickname:

1) Johnny Bower   a) Ukey

2) Frank Brimsek   b) The China Wall

3) Alex Connell   c) Shrimp

4) Terry Sawchuk   d) Mr. Zero

5) Roy Worters   e) The Ottawa Fireman

Name the New York Rangers netminder who surrendered Bill Mosienko's three goals in 21 seconds:

a) Chuck Rayner   c) Marcel Paille

b) Lorne Anderson   d) Emile Francis

On February 20, 1930, Clint Benedict became the first goalie to wear a mask in a game when he donned a leather face shield to try and protect a broken nose. What other important innovation was Benedict a part of pioneering?

1-b: Bower's age and impenetrability resulted in the nickname the "China Wall."

2-d: Brimsek was dubbed "Mr. Zero" after twice running up streaks of three straight shutouts during his first month with the Boston Bruins in 1938–39.

3-e: Connell was known as the "Ottawa Fireman" both because of his off-season job as a fireman and for putting out the fire of opposing marksmen.

4-a: Sawchuk was called "Ukey" because of his Ukrainian heritage.

5-c: "Shrimp" Worters stood just five foot three.

Lorne Anderson played only three games in the NHL. His third and final appearance came on March 23, 1952, the last night of the 1951–52 season. That night he allowed Mosienko to score three times in 21 seconds midway through the third period as the Blackhawks rallied to beat the Rangers 7–6.

In the early days of hockey, goaltenders were required to remain on their feet at all times. This rule was still in force when the NHL began operating in 1917–18, but Benedict's habit of "accidentally" falling on the puck caused a change in the ruling during the league's first season.

Match the goaltender who was known by his nickname to his proper first name:

1) Turk Broda   a) Clarence

2) Dolly Dolson   b) Walter

3) Chico Resch   c) Lorne

4) Tiny Thompson   d) Glenn

5) Gump Worsley   e) Cecil

Name the netminder who led the NHL in wins, shutouts, and goals–against average during both the regular season and the playoffs in 1942–43, yet never won another game in his NHL career.

a) Frank McCool   c) Johnny Mowers

b) Alfie Moore   d) Mike Karakas

1-b: Walter Broda earned his nickname as a youngster either because of the way his neck reddened when he was angry or sunburned (depending on the story) or because his freckles made his skin look like a turkey egg.

2-a: Clarence "Dolly" Dolson played for Detroit back when the team was known as the Cougars and the Falcons. "Dolly" was short for Dolson.

3-d: Glenn Resch was nicknamed "Chico" because of his resemblance to Freddie Prinze, star of the 1970s TV show Chico and the Man.

4-e: Cecil Thompson was known as "Tiny" due to the miniscule size of his goals-against average.

5-c: Lorne Worsley became known as "Gump" as a youngster because of his resemblance to a comic strip character of the same name.

c: Johnny Mowers won the Vezina Trophy and led Detroit to the Stanley Cup in 1942–43, then enlisted for military duty in World War II. He played hockey in England for a year after the war, then returned to Detroit briefly for seven games in 1946–47. He went 0–6–1. Mowers retired after a short stint in the minors the following year.

Name the future Hall of Fame goaltender who led the NHL in shutouts in 1966–67, 1967–68, and 1970–71.

a) Gump Worsley   c) Eddie Giacomin

b) Tony Esposito   d) Glenn Hall

Match the goaltender to his playoff accomplishment:

1) Gerry McNeil   a) most consecutive playoff wins

2) Grant Fuhr   b) most consecutive wins in the finals

3) Tom Barrasso   c) gave up two Stanley Cup winners in overtime

4) Terry Sawchuk   d) first to win 16 games in one playoff year

5) Ken Dryden   e) fewest goals allowed in a best-of-seven final

Three goaltenders shared netminding duties in Montreal when Ken Dryden sat out the entire 1973–74 season. How many can you name?

c: Eddie Giacomin had a long stay in the minors before reaching the NHL with the New York Rangers in 1965–66. One year later, he led the league with nine shutouts. He topped the NHL with eight shutouts in 1967–68. He shared the Vezina Trophy with Gilles Villemure after leading the league with eight shutouts again in 1970–71.

1-c: McNeil allowed Bill Barilko's overtime winner in 1951 and Tony Leswick's double overtime winner in 1954.

2-d: Fuhr was the first goalie to win 16 games in one playoff year when the Oilers won the Stanley Cup in 1988.

3-a: Barrasso won 11 straight games to close out the 1992 playoffs, then won three in a row to open the postseason in 1993.

4-e: Sawchuk allowed only two goals in four games when the Red Wings swept the Canadiens in 1952.

5-b: Dryden was in net for the Canadiens when they won a record 10 straight games in the finals between 1976 and 1978.

Wayne Thomas served as Montreal's number-one netminder in Dryden's absence, posting a record of 23–12–5 with a 2.76 average in 43 games. Michel "Bunny" Larocque went 15–8–2 with a 2.89 average in 27 games. Michel Plasse was 7–4–2 with a 4.08 average in 15 games.

Tony Esposito was one of the first hockey stars to emerge from the U.S. college ranks. Where did he go to school?

a) Ferris State

b) Michigan Tech

c) Notre Dame

d) Ohio State

What NHL team originally selected Ken Dryden as a 17-year-old in the 1964 NHL Amateur Draft?

a) Toronto

b) Boston

c) New York

d) Chicago

Who was the netminder that Punch Imlach mocked as a "Junior B goalie" during the 1967 Stanley Cup final between Toronto and Montreal?

Tony Esposito starred at Michigan Tech, earning NCAA West First-Team All-American honors in 1965, 1966, and 1967.

Dryden was selected 14th overall (of just 24 picks made) by the Boston Bruins in 1964, but his rights were soon dealt to Montreal. Dryden entered Cornell University in 1965 and starred there for four seasons before joining the Canadian national team in 1969–70. He finally turned pro in 1970–71 and led the Canadiens to the Stanley Cup after being summoned from the minors late that season.

Rogie Vachon was called up to the Canadiens midway through the 1966–67 season, and though he was riding a hot streak, Imlach hoped to face the rookie in the finals instead of veteran Gump Worsley. According to Terry Harper, Imlach's attacks on Vachon made Toe Blake determined to prove Montreal could beat Toronto with the youngster in net. It turned out that they couldn't and by the time Blake turned to Worsley in game six, it was too late.

This one-time Toronto Maple Leafs goaltender is the only player who was selected in both the 1967 Expansion Draft and the 1979 Expansion Draft. Can you name him?

Patrick Roy's 448th victory on October 17, 2000, moved him past Terry Sawchuk as the winningest goaltender in NHL history. Put these other 400-game winners in order of their career victories, starting with the most:

a) Tony Esposito   c) Glenn Hall

b) Jacques Plante   d) Grant Fuhr

Only one goalie in NHL history has had to face the pressure of game seven three times in one playoff year. Who was it?

a) Ken Dryden   c) Mike Richter

b) Ron Hextall   d) Felix Potvin

Doug Favell was taken by Philadelphia from Boston in the 1967 Expansion Draft. He was traded to Toronto in 1973, and later sold to the Colorado Rockies in 1976. Colorado left Favell unprotected in 1979. He was chosen by the Edmonton Oilers, but decided to retire.

b) Jacques Plante, 435

a) Tony Esposito, 423

c) Glenn Hall, 407

d) Grant Fuhr, 403

d: The 1992–93 Toronto Maple Leafs are the only team to play three seven-game series in one playoff year. Felix Potvin picked up the win as the Leafs edged Detroit 4–3 in overtime to win the first series, then blanked St. Louis in a 6–0 rout to close out round two. In the third round, Potvin and the Leafs dropped a 5–4 heartbreaker to Wayne Gretzky and the Kings to close out a run of 21 playoff games in 42 nights.

Match the current NHL netminder with the first year he played in the league:

1) Ed Belfour	a) 1987–88
2) Sean Burke	b) 1988–89
3) Curtis Joseph	c) 1989–90
4) Trevor Kidd	d) 1990–91
5) Damian Rhodes	e) 1991–92

I was a Stanley Cup champion with the New York Rangers and the Toronto Maple Leafs, and won the Vezina Trophy with the Chicago Blackhawks in 1934–35. I have 201 career victories and a 2.04 lifetime goals-against average. My 73 career shutouts currently rank eighth in NHL history, yet I am not in the Hockey Hall of Fame. Who am I?

1-b: Belfour played 23 games for Chicago in 1988–89 and nine games in the playoffs the following year. He was still considered a rookie when he became a star and won the Calder and Vezina trophies in 1990–91.

2-a: Burke broke in with the New Jersey Devils late in the 1987–88 season, after playing for Canada at the Olympics.

3-c: Joseph was signed by the St. Louis Blues in 1989 after a year at the University of Wisconsin. He spent most of the 1989–90 season in the minors, but did play 15 games with the Blues that year.

4-e: After a sensational junior career and a season with Canada's national team, Kidd broke in with the Calgary Flames after the 1992 Albertville Olympics. He spent the entire 1992–93 season in the minors before returning to the NHL in 1993–94.

5-d: Rhodes played one game for the Toronto Maple Leafs in 1990–91, then spent two more years in the minors before returning to the NHL in 1993–94.

L orne Chabot

Put the following goaltenders in order of career victories, starting with the fewest:

a) Andy Moog   c) Ron Hextall

b) Billy Smith   d) Bernie Parent

Who set the single-season record for most games played by a goaltender in 1995–96, and how many games did he play?

Who was the last goaltender to play in every game for his team in a single season?

d) Bernie Parent, 271

c) Ron Hextall, 296

b) Billy Smith, 305

a) Andy Moog, 372

Many people thought Grant Fuhr was washed up when he signed with St. Louis for the 1995–96 season. He would prove his skeptics wrong, playing 76 consecutive games before being sidelined by a knee injury. In all, Fuhr played 79 games that year. He suffered a serious knee injury in the playoffs, but returned to play 73 games in 1996–97.

During much of the Original Six era, it was commonplace for goaltenders to play all 70 games in a season. The last to do so was Roger Crozier with the Detroit Red Wings in 1964–65. Crozier, however, was replaced by Carl Wetzel for parts of two games that season. The last goaltender to play every minute of every game for his team was Eddie Johnston of the Boston Bruins in 1963–64.

Who was the last goalie from the Original Six era to still be active in the NHL?

a) Bernie Parent

c) Rogie Vachon

b) Ed Giacomin

d) Gerry Cheevers

Match the goaltender to his accomplishment:

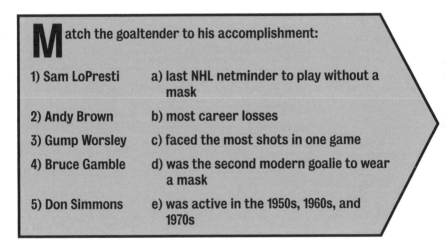

1) Sam LoPresti	a) last NHL netminder to play without a mask
2) Andy Brown	b) most career losses
3) Gump Worsley	c) faced the most shots in one game
4) Bruce Gamble	d) was the second modern goalie to wear a mask
5) Don Simmons	e) was active in the 1950s, 1960s, and 1970s

What was significant about the shutout recorded by Pete LoPresti on February 8, 1975?

c: Rogie Vachon entered the NHL with the Montreal Canadiens in 1966–67 and played his final season in 1981–82 when he was in goal for 38 games with Detroit. Gerry Cheevers played his first NHL game in 1961–62 and was still active in 1979–80. Bernie Parent's first season was 1965–66 and his last was 1978–79. Eddie Giacomin broke in in 1965–66 and played through the 1977–78 season.

1-c: LoPresti faced 83 shots in one game on March 4, 1941. Though he made 80 saves, his Chicago Blackhawks dropped a 3–2 decision to Boston.

2-a: Brown played without a mask for three seasons with the Red Wings and Penguins from 1971–72 to 1973–74. Gump Worsley donned a mask in 1973–74.

3-b: Worsley lost 352 games in his 21-year career, one more than Gilles Meloche. He also won 335 games.

4-e: Gamble is one of seven goalies active in these three decades. So was Gump Worsley. The others are Jacques Plante, Terry Sawchuk, Glenn Hall, Charlie Hodge, and Johnny Bower.

5-d: Simmons first wore a mask on December 13, 1959, five weeks after Jacques Plante first wore his in a game, though he did not always wear one after that.

When Minnesota North Stars rookie Pete LoPresti blanked Philadelphia 5–0 it made him and Sam LoPresti the first father-and-son combination to record NHL shutouts.

Patrick Roy surpassed Terry Sawchuk as the NHL's all-time winningest goaltender, but whose record did Sawchuk break back in 1961–62?

Which goalie holds the single-season record for wins and how many games did he win?

Prior to the presentation of the Jennings Trophy in 1981–82, the Vezina Trophy was awarded to the goalie or goalies on the team that allowed the fewest goals against. Match the following Vezina Trophy winners to the player with whom he shared the honor:

1) Ken Dryden   a) Tony Esposito

2) Bernie Parent   b) Denis Dejordy

3) Tony Esposito   c) Charlie Hodge

4) Glenn Hall   d) Gary Smith

5) Gump Worsley   e) Michel Larocque

When Terry Sawchuk recorded his 331st victory in 1961–62, he surpassed Harry Lumley as the NHL's all-time win leader.

Bernie Parent broke Terry Sawchuk's single-season record of 44 victories when he recorded 47 (47–13–12) in 1973–74. Sawchuk had recorded 44 in both 1950–51 and 1951–52. Parent surpassed his two-season win total when he recorded 44 wins of his own in 1974–75.

1-e: Montreal teammates Dryden and Larocque shared the trophy in 1976–77, 1977–78, and 1978–79. Dryden had won it by himself in 1972–73 and 1975–76.

2-a: Parent shared the Vezina Trophy with Esposito in 1973–74 after both the Flyers and the Canadiens allowed a league-low 164 goals in 78 games. It's the only time in history that players on two different teams shared the award.

3-d: Chicago teammates Esposito and Smith shared the Vezina Trophy in 1971–72. Previously, Espo had won it by himself in 1969–70.

4-b: Chicago teammates Hall and Dejordy shared the trophy in 1966–67. Hall later shared the Vezina with Jacques Plante in St. Louis in 1968–69. Previously, he had won it by himself in 1962–63.

5-c: Montreal teammates Worsley and Hodge shared the Vezina in 1965–66. Worsley later shared it with Rogie Vachon in 1967–68. Charlie Hodge won it by himself in 1963–64.

Chapter **12**

The International Game

The history of hockey in Europe dates back nearly as far as it does in North America. Many of the European nations that would become prominent in the sport learned the necessary skills while playing bandy, a game of field hockey on ice that had developed widespread appeal across Europe by the 1890s. In the early days of European hockey, England, France, Germany, and Switzerland were the powerhouses, but as the 20th century progressed, Czechoslovakia and Sweden began to dominate.

Despite the lengthy history of the game in Europe, Canadian teams were easily able to defeat their European opponents once Olympic and World Championship tournaments began in the

1920s and '30s. In fact, Canada could send almost any championship amateur team to Europe and expect to come home with a gold medal . . . until the Soviets made their first appearance at the World Championships in 1954. That year, the USSR stunned Canada's East York Lyndhursts with a 7–2 victory in the decisive game.

Though Canadian club teams would have success against the Soviets for the rest of the 1950s, the USSR began to dominate in the 1960s. Father David Bauer organized the first Canadian national team program in the mid 1960s, but Canada withdrew from international hockey in 1969 after a flip-flop by the International Ice Hockey Federation over the use of professional players. The historic 1972 Canada-Russia Summit series, when top NHL stars took on the Soviet national team for the first time, paved the way for Canada's return to international hockey and for future tournaments like the Canada Cup and the World Cup of Hockey. Professional players began to compete at the Olympics in the 1980s, and by 1998 an agreement with the IIHF had opened the Winter Games to full participation by NHL players.

How many seconds were remaining when Paul Henderson scored the game-winning goal for Team Canada in 1972? What was the final score of the game?

Team Canada had a 35-man roster in 1972, but only 20 men could dress per game. Paul Henderson was one of only seven Canadians who played in all eight games. How many others can you name?

Ken Dryden and Tony Esposito shared goaltending duties for Team Canada in 1972. Can you name the third-string netminder who saw no action during the series?

Paul Henderson scored at 19:26 of the third period, meaning just 34 seconds were left when he gave Team Canada a 6–5 win and a 4–3–1 victory in the eight-game series.

Phil Esposito, Bobby Clarke, Yvan Cournoyer, Brad Park, Gary Bergman, and Ron Ellis also played all eight games for Team Canada. Bill White, Pete Mahovlich, Guy Lapointe, and Pat Stapleton dressed for seven. Jean Ratelle, Rod Gilbert, J. P. Parise, and Frank Mahovlich played in six games. No one else played in more than four.

Eddie Johnston was Canada's third-string goaltender. The Soviets had three backups for Vladislav Tretiak, who played all eight games in the series. The main backup was Alexander Sidelnikov, who dressed for five games but saw no action.

Team Canada did not have a captain in 1972, going instead with four alternate captains (Phil Esposito, Jean Ratelle, Stan Mikita, and Frank Mahovlich). Who wore the "K" as captain of the Soviets?

Through the 1998 Winter Olympics, the Soviets/Russians have won eight gold medals. Canada has five and the United States two. Three other teams have won the gold medal once. Which one of these is not one of them:

a) Sweden   c) Great Britain

b) Finland   d) Czech Republic

Three members of Team Canada 1972 suited up again in 1974 when a group of all-stars from the World Hockey Association took on the Soviets. Can you name them?

Boris Mikhailov was the longtime captain of the Soviet national team. In addition to the 1972 Summit Series, he played at the Olympics in 1972, 1976, and 1980 and at 11 World Championships.

b: Finland's best Olympic result is a silver medal in 1988. The Finns won bronze in 1994 and 1998. Sweden won gold in 1994, while the Czechs won in 1998. Great Britain won the gold medal in hockey in 1936 with a team composed mainly of players who had been born in England but raised and trained in Canada.

Paul Henderson, Frank Mahovlich, and Pat Stapleton all played for Team Canada 1974. This time the Soviets took the series, winning four games to Canada's one with three ending in ties.

Phil Esposito was the leading scorer of the 1972 Canada–Russia series with seven goals and six assists. Paul Henderson had seven goals and three assists. Which player led the Soviets in scoring with seven goals and four assists?

a) Alexander Yakushev

b) Valeri Kharlamov

c) Vladimir Petrov

d) Alexander Maltsev

Put the following events in chronological order, starting with the earliest:

a) Soviets win world title

b) Sweden wins world title

c) Czechs win world title

d) United States wins world title

The coach of the 1972 Soviet squad had been the national team's first captain. Can you name him?

a: Alexander Yakushev was the Soviet's top scorer. Valeri Kharlamov and Vladimir Petrov both had three goals and four assists. Alexander Maltsev had no goals, but did collect five assists.

d) The U.S. won the World Championships for the first time in 1933, beating Canada's National "Sea Fleas" 2–1 in overtime in the deciding game.

c) Czechoslovakia won the World Championships for the first time in 1947. No Canadian team was present that year, but the Czechs beat the Sudbury Wolves en route to winning the 1949 World Championship.

a) The Soviets won their first World Championship at their first tournament in 1954.

b) Sweden won its first world title in 1957, beating the Soviets in Moscow at a tournament without a Canadian team. When Sweden won again at Colorado Springs in 1962, a Canadian team was present—but the Soviets were not.

Vsevolod Bobrov was the first Soviet superstar, leading his teams to seven league titles while scoring 254 goals in 130 league games. He competed internationally from 1954 to 1957, winning a world championship and an Olympic gold medal. He took over as coach of the Soviet national team in 1972 and held the job until 1974.

Match the following Canadian club team to the year it won the Olympic or World Championship:

1) Edmonton Mercurys   a) 1939

2) Penticton Vees   b) 1948

3) RCAF Flyers   c) 1952

4) Trail Smoke Eaters   d) 1955

5) Whitby Dunlops   e) 1958

After his heroics with the "Miracle on Ice" United States team at the 1980 Lake Placid Winter Olympics, Jim Craig broke into the NHL with which team?

1-c: The Mercurys went 7–0–1 at the 1952 Olympics, tying the Americans 3–3 despite outshooting them 58–13. To date, the Mercurys (who also won the 1950 World Championship) are the last Canadian team to win Olympic gold.

2-d: After the USSR beat Canada to win the world title in 1954, the Penticton Vees were determined to bring the title back home. They romped to a perfect 8–0 record in 1955, including a 5–0 win over the Soviets.

3-b: The RCAF Flyers won Olympic gold in 1948 based on goal differential. Both Canada and Czechoslovakia were undefeated, including a scoreless tie against one another, at the Olympics in St. Moritz, Switzerland.

4-a: The Smoke Eaters, who would later become the last Canadian amateur team to win the World Championship in 1961, first won the world title back in 1939.

5-e: The Dunlops had beaten the Soviets when they made their first appearance in Canada in November 1957, then beat them at the 1958 World Championships.

Jim Craig had been selected by the Atlanta Flames with the 72nd pick in the 1977 NHL Draft, after his first of three seasons at Boston University. He made his NHL debut with the Flames shortly after the Olympics, going 1–2–1 with a 3.79 goals-against average in four games. He was traded to Boston the following season and went 9–7–6 with a 3.68 average in 23 games. He did not play in the NHL again until suiting up for three games with the Minnesota North Stars in 1983–84. His final NHL record was 11–10–7 with a 3.78 average in 30 career games.

Who scored the winning goal when the USA beat the USSR in Lake Placid and what was the score of the game?

Name the member of the 1980 "Miracle on Ice" team whose father and uncle had both been members of the 1960 gold-medal winning team.

This hero of the U.S. gold medal team at the 1960 Squaw Valley Olympics also had a brief NHL career, though he did play 16 seasons as a pro and went on to become an NHL scout. Can you name this netminder?

Captain Mike Eruzione scored midway through the third period to give the Americans a 4–3 victory over the Soviets. Though many people remember this game as the gold-medal winner, the Americans actually had to beat Finland two days later (they won 4–2) to be guaranteed the gold.

Dave Christian was a forward who was converted to defense by USA coach Herb Brooks. He led the team with eight assists at the 1980 Olympic tournament. His father Bill and uncle Roger were longtime U.S. amateur stars.

Jack McCartan had been an All-American at the University of Minnesota and was a member of the 1959 U.S. national team. Still, he was a late addition to the 1960 Olympic squad. Then, like Jim Craig 20 years later, it was largely due to his brilliant play that the United States captured the gold medal. McCartan played four games for the New York Rangers later that season, then eight games with the club in 1960–61. After years in the minors, he later played in the WHA.

Which American player was the leading scorer at the 1980 Olympics?

Name the member of the American team who followed up his 1980 gold medal with a Stanley Cup championship that year.

Darryl Sittler scored the winning goal in overtime when Canada defeated Czechoslovakia to win the inaugural Canada Cup tournament. Put the following events in order of when they occured in the Canada Cup, starting with the earliest:

a) Canada beats Sweden in final

b) USSR beats Canada in final

c) Gretzky sets scoring record

d) Canada goes undefeated

Mark Johnson led the Olympic tournament with 11 points (five goals, six assists) in seven games. He went on to play with five teams over 11 seasons in the NHL and later played in Italy and Austria before getting into coaching like his father, U.S. hockey legend Bob Johnson.

Ken Morrow joined the New York Islanders after the Olympics and not only won the Stanley Cup that year, but for four years in a row.

b) The Soviets beat Canada 8–1 in the one-game final of the 1981 Canada Cup.

a) After Mike Bossy's overtime goal sunk the Soviets in the semifinals of the 1984 Canada Cup, Canada went on to sweep Sweden in the best-of-three final.

c) Wayne Gretzky had a record 21 points in nine games during the 1987 Canada Cup. He had three goals and 18 assists, including one on Mario Lemieux's winning goal in the final seconds of the final game.

d) Canada had six wins and two ties at the 1991 Canada Cup, the only time in tournament history that a team went undefeated.

Once in the 1970s and once in the '80s, the NHL replaced its All-Star Game with an international tournament. What where these called?

Name the future NHL star who set a World Junior Championships scoring record with 31 points in just seven games in 1992–93:

a) Paul Kariya

b) Eric Lindros

c) Peter Forsberg

d) Markus Naslund

Name the only Swedish player to score 50 goals in the NHL.

The Challenge Cup was held at Madison Square Garden in February 1979 and pitted a team of NHL All-Stars against the Soviet Union. The NHLers won game one and led game two 4–2 until the Soviets rallied for a 5–4 victory. In game three, the Soviets skated to a 6–0 victory. Rendez-Vous '87 in Quebec City was a two-game exhibition. The NHLers won game one 4–3 and the Soviets took game two 5–3.

c: Peter Forsberg had seven goals and 24 assists in seven games for Sweden at the 1993 World Junior Championships. Teammate Markus Naslund had 13 goals and 11 assists. Both were joined on the tournament all-star team by Paul Kariya, who had just two goals and six assists but led Canada to its fifth straight Junior title. Sweden finished second.

A former Swedish scoring champion, Hakan Loob scored 50 goals (and had 56 assists) for the Calgary Flames in 1987–88. He returned to Sweden after helping the Flames win the Stanley Cup in 1989 and led the Swedish league in scoring again three times in the next four years. Sweden's Kent Nilsson reached the 40-goal plateau three times with the Flames in the 1980s, including a high of 49 goals in 1980–81.

The 1998 Winter Olympics marked the first time that the NHL took time off from the season to allow its players to compete at the Olympics. Match the following NHL players to the feat they accomplished in Nagano:

1) Pavel Bure   a) scored the gold medal–winning goal

2) Saku Koivu   b) led the Olympics in scoring

3) Teemu Selanne   c) led the Olympics in goals scored

4) Robert Reichel   d) led the Olympics in assists

5) Petr Svoboda   e) scored against Canada in the shootout

Which one of the three Stastny brothers was the only one to be drafted by an NHL team?

1-c: Bure was the top goal scorer at the Olympics with nine goals in six games. He scored five times in Russia's semifinal win over Finland.

2-d: Koivu led the Olympics with eight assists in six games. His 10 points tied him for top spot with Teemu Selanne.

3-b: Selanne had four goals and six assists to share the Olympic scoring title with Saku Koivu. Selanne's ranked first because he scored more goals.

4-e: Reichel scored the only goal in the shootout that gave the Czechs a win over Canada in the semifinals. Patrick Roy stopped the next four shots, but Dominik Hasek blanked Theo Fleury, Ray Bourque, Joe Nieuwendyk, Eric Lindros, and Brendan Shanahan.

5-a: Petr Svoboda scored the only goal as the Czech Republic beat the Russians 1–0 in the gold-medal game.

Anton Stastny was actually drafted twice. The Philadelphia Flyers selected him 198th overall in 1978, but when they could not sign him within the year, he became eligible to be drafted again in 1979. This time, the Quebec Nordiques chose him 83rd overall and signed both him and Peter when they defected in the summer of 1980. Marian Stastny joined his brothers in Quebec the following year.

With 601 goals and 1,398 points, Jari Kurri is the highest-scoring European player in NHL history. What team was Kurri with when he became the first European player to score 600 goals?

Name the first Soviet-trained player to play in the NHL.

Seven members of Team Canada did not see any action during the 1972 series. How many can you name?

Jari Kurri was with the Colorado Avalanche for his final NHL season of 1997–98. He also played for his native Finland at the Olympics that year. After 10 seasons with Edmonton and four-plus years with Los Angeles, Kurri bounced around over his final two-plus seasons, playing with the Rangers, Anaheim, and Colorado.

Viktor Nechayev played three games with the Los Angeles Kings in 1982–83. Though not an elite-level player, Nechayev had played nine seasons in the Soviet Union when he met and married an American student traveling in the USSR. He was later allowed to go to the States, and convinced the Kings to give him a tryout. They were impressed enough to select him (132nd overall) in the 1982 NHL Entry Draft, but he spent most of the 1982–83 season in the minors. The following year, he played hockey in Germany. The first player to play in the NHL with the permission of the Soviet Hockey Federation was Sergei Priakin, who joined the Calgary Flames in 1988–89.

In addition to Eddie Johnston, Marcel Dionne, Brian Glennie, Jocelyn Guevremont, Rick Martin, Dale Tallon, and Bobby Orr (who was recovering from knee surgery) did not play a single game for Team Canada. Mickey Redmond played just one game, while six other players dressed for only two.